INTERPRETIVE INTERACTIONISM

Second Edition

Norman K. Denzin

Applied Social Research Methods Series
Volume 16

Sage Publications
International Educational and Professional Publisher
Thousand Oaks ▪ London ▪ New Delhi

For information:

Sage Publications, Inc.
2455 Teller Road
Thousand Oaks, California 91320
E-mail: order@sagepub.com

Sage Publications Ltd.
6 Bonhill Street
London EC2A 4PU
United Kingdom

Sage Publications India Pvt. Ltd.
M-32 Market
Greater Kailash I
New Delhi 110 048 India

Printed in the United States of America

Library of Congress Cataloging-in-Publication Data

Denzin, Norman K.
    Interpretive interactionism / Norman K. Denzin.— 2nd ed.
        p. cm. — (Applied social research methods series ; v. 16)
    Includes bibliographical references and index.
    ISBN 0-7619-1513-3 (hard : alk.) — ISBN 0-7619-1514-1 (pbk. : Alk.)
    1. Sociology—Methodology. 2. Social interaction. 3.
Sociology—Biographical methods. 4. Symbolic interactionism. I. Title.
II. Series.
    HM511 .D45 2001
    301'.01—dc21   2001002979

01   02   03   04   05   06   10   9   8   7   6   5   4   3   2   1

Acquiring Editor:	C. Deborah Laughton
Editorial Assistants:	Veronica Novak and Ester Marcelino
Production Editor:	Claudia A. Hoffman
Copy Editor:	Judy Selhorst
Typesetter:	Denyse Dunn
Indexer:	Molly Hall

Contents

Preface

In 1989, when the first edition of *Interpretive Interactionism* was published, the rather considerable social science literature on qualitative research methods did not contain any extended treatment of the "interpretive," existential point of view (see Douglas & Johnson, 1977; Kotarba & Fontana, 1984). Nor had there been any serious attempts to apply this perspective to the study of personal troubles and turning-point moments in the lives of interacting individuals. With *Interpretive Interactionism*, I attempted to fill that void.[1] That volume was, and remains, designed to provide students and scholars in the human disciplines with a relatively accessible description of the critical, existential, interpretive approach as it has been practiced by myself and others.[2]

This new edition carries forth the themes of the first edition. Since 1989, there has been an explosion in the field of qualitative research. Interpretive interactionism is part of that explosion. Indeed, it is part of a larger reformist movement that began at least two decades earlier, in the 1970s (Schwandt, 2000, p. 189). The interpretive and critical paradigms, in their several forms, are central to this movement, as are complex epistemological and ethical criticisms of traditional social science research. The field of qualitative inquiry now has its own journals, scientific associations, conferences, and faculty positions (Denzin & Lincoln, 2000c, p. x). The movement has made significant inroads into many social science disciplines, including communication, sociology, anthropology, medicine, social work, advertising, marketing, and consumer research.

The transformations in qualitative inquiry that gained momentum in the 1990s continue into the new century. Today, few look back with skepticism on the narrative turn. Many have told their tales from the field. Further, it is now understood that writing is not an innocent practice. Men and women write culture differently. Sociologists and anthropologists continue to explore new ways of composing ethnography, and more than a few are writing fiction, drama, performance texts, and ethnographic poetry. Social science journals are holding fiction contests. Civic journalists are experimenting with various forms of critical ethnography.

The appeal of a critical cultural studies across the social sciences and the humanities increases. Some term this the "seventh moment" of inquiry (Denzin & Lincoln, 2000b, pp. 2, 12).[3] This is a period of ferment and explosion. It is defined by breaks from the past, a focus on previously silenced voices, a turn to performance texts, and a concern with moral discourse, with critical conversations about democracy, race, gender, class, nation, freedom, and community (Lincoln & Denzin, 2000, p. 1048).

In the seventh moment, at the beginning of the 21st century, there is a pressing demand to show how the practices of critical, interpretive qualitative research can help change the world in positive ways. It is necessary to examine new ways of making the practices of critical qualitative inquiry central to the workings of a free democratic society. These are the issues that interpretive interactionism attempts to address.

In *The Sociological Imagination,* C. Wright Mills (1959) challenged scholars in the human disciplines to develop a point of view and a methodological attitude that would allow them to examine how the private troubles of individuals, which occur within the immediate world of experience, are connected to public issues and to public responses to these troubles (see also Agger, 2000, p. 265; Lemert, 1997b, p. 161). Mills's sociological imagination was biographical, interactional, and historical.

Mills understood that human beings live in a secondhand world. Existence is not determined solely by interaction, or by social acts. Mills (1963) put this forcefully: "The consciousness of human beings does not determine their existence; nor does their existence determine their consciousness. Between the human consciousness and material existence stand communications, and designs, patterns, and values which influence decisively such consciousness as they have" (p. 375). Humans have no direct access to reality. Reality, as it is known, is mediated by symbolic representations, by narrative texts, and by televisual and cinematic structures that stand between the person and the so-called real world. We can never capture this world directly; we can only study representations of it. We study the ways people represent their experiences to themselves and to others. Experience can be represented in multiple ways, including through rituals, myths, stories, performances, films, songs, memoirs, and autobiographies. Experiences come in multiple forms: problematic, routine, ritual, liminal, epiphanic, turning point (see below).

Mills wanted his sociology to make a difference in the lives that people lead. He challenged individuals to take history into their own hands. He wanted to bend the structures of capitalism to the ideologies of radical democracy. Despite the enormous influence of Mills's work, there has never been a methodological discussion of how his theory and method might be put in place. This book continues Mills's project.

The perspective is termed *interpretive interactionism.* By this rather awkward phrase, I refer to the attempt to make the problematic lived experiences of ordinary people available to the reader. The interactionist interprets these worlds, their meanings, and their representations. The research methods of this approach include performance texts, autoethnography, poetry, fiction, open-ended and creative interviewing, document analysis, semiotics, life history, life story, personal experience and self-story construction, participant observation, and thick description.

The term *interpretive interactionism,* as the above list of methods suggests, signifies an attempt to join traditional symbolic interactionist thought (Blumer, 1969; Denzin, 1992) with critical forms of interpretive inquiry, including reflexive participant observation and postmodern and literary ethnography (Angrosino & Mays de Pérez, 2000; Kincheloe & McLaren, 2000; Richardson, 2000; Tedlock, 2000); feminist, cultural studies, and critical race theory (Frow & Morris, 2000; Ladson-Billings, 2000; Olesen, 2000); queer theory (Gamson, 2000); naturalistic, constructivist, and case studies (Lincoln & Guba, 2000; Stake, 2000); poetics, life stories, and *testimonios* (Beverley, 2000; Brady, 2000; Tierney, 2000); creative and active interviewing (Holstein & Gubrium, 1995); participatory action research (Kemmis & McTaggart, 2000); narrative, semiotic, interpretive, and Foucauldian structural discourse analysis (Gubrium & Holstein, 2000); and the interpretive, hermeneutic, phenomenological works of Heidegger (1927/1962, 1982) and Gadamer (1975).

Those interested in acquiring some familiarity with the background of the present book might consult some of my earlier work: *The Research Act* (Denzin, 1970, 1978, 1989b), *On Understanding Emotion* (Denzin, 1984a), my three studies of the American alcoholic (Denzin, 1987a, 1987b, 1987c), *Interpretive Ethnography* (Denzin, 1997), and my recently completed *Reading Race: Hollywood and the Cinema of Racial Violence* (Denzin, 2001).

THE ORGANIZATION OF THIS WORK

This volume is organized into eight chapters. In Chapter 1, I discuss the issues surrounding interpretive criteria in the seventh moment as well as the narrative and performance turns in the social sciences today, offering some examples from my recent work. In Chapter 2, I define interpretive interactionism, laying out its basic assumptions and terms. I discuss the concept of epiphany in great detail in Chapter 2, and compare interpretive interactionism to the progressive-regressive method of Sartre, feminist standpoint epistemologies, and Foucault's arguments about power, discourse, truth, and knowledge.

In Chapter 3, I address how meaningful, biographical experience is secured and discuss selves, narratives, and sacred places in the culture. Chapter 4 outlines the steps in the interpretive process. In Chapter 5, I examine how researchers situate interpretive studies in the "ethnoscapes" of daily life; this includes discussion of multisited ethnographies and mobile ethnographers. In Chapter 6, I address thick description as a narrative strategy, building on Geertz's arguments first made in 1973. I also review contemporary discourse on the uses and forms of thick description. In Chapter 7, I show how interpretation is done, giving special attention to the performance of interpretation. I also explore alternative writing forms, including poetry, layered texts, and short stories. In Chapter 8, where I summarize and present my main conclusions, I emphasize the existential nature of this research and locate it in the late postmodern moment. A glossary of terms follows Chapter 8.

Three assumptions organize this work. First, in the world of human experience, there is only interpretation. Second, it is a worthy goal for researchers to attempt to make these interpretations available to others. By so doing, they can create understanding, and with better understanding come better applied programs for addressing the major social issues of our day. Third, all interpretations are unfinished and inconclusive. So it is with this book. It remains for readers to form their own interpretations of this project that I call interpretive interactionism.

Acknowledgments

I would like to thank the following persons for their assistance on this project. C. Deborah Laughton at Sage Publications arranged for the appearance of a second edition of *Interpretive Interactionism* in 1997. She has been waiting patiently ever since. Because this revision leans on the first edition, it is appropriate that I thank once again those who were involved in the initial project. Leonard Bickman originally proposed the idea and guided me through proposals and successive revisions. Without him, the first edition would never have been written. During the writing of the first edition I was subjected to considerable pain at the hands of Debra J. Rog and the late Carl J. Couch. They destroyed my first and second drafts, and I think this became a better book because of what they did. Conversations with David R. Maines clarified many of the ideas in Chapter 6. Robert Stake's comments on an earlier draft served to sharpen my position on the topic of qualitative evaluation studies.

Jack Bratich is the person who made this revision possible. He traced down obscure references, recovered lost computer files, and kept everything moving forward. Jack and Ruoyun Bai put the bibliography in order, and Mark Nimkoff and Michael Elavsky proofread the manuscript. At Sage, Astrid Virding aided in the search for the lost files. Also at Sage, I thank Judy Selhorst for careful copyediting, Claudia Hoffman for shepherding this book through the production process, and Molly Hall for preparing the index.

As always, I thank Katherine E. Ryan, my wife. Her good humor helped me stay with this project.

— Norman K. Denzin
Champaign, Illinois

NOTES

1. A companion work, *Interpretive Biography* (Denzin, 1989a) was published in the same year. That work went more deeply into the biographical, life story implications of this interpretive approach. Nearly 10 years later, *Interpretive Ethnography* (Denzin, 1997) extended these earlier works, giving particular attention to the many ways we write culture.

These works framed my contributions to the two editions of the *Handbook of Qualitative Research* (Denzin & Lincoln, 1994, 2000a).

2. Interpretive interactionism, as a perspective and method, has received considerable interest and attention in the social science community (see Carspecken, 1996; Charmaz, 2000; Coffey, 1999; Creswell, 1998; Flick, 1998; Hollway & Jefferson, 2000; Schwandt, 1994).

3. In previous work, Yvonna Lincoln and I have defined the seven moments of inquiry, all of which operate in the present, as follows: the traditional (1900-1950), the modernist (1950-1970), blurred genres (1970-1986), the crisis of representation (1986-1990), the postmodern or experimental (1990 to 1995), the postexperimental (1995-2000), and the future (2000-) (Denzin & Lincoln, 2000b, p. 2).

1

Interpretive Criteria
in the Seventh Moment

This chapter presents interpretive criteria in the seventh moment. The following topics are discussed: (a) when to use the interpretive approach; (b) moral, ethical, and aesthetic criteria of evaluation; (c) moral criticism and taking sides; (e) the blurring of interpretive genres; (f) civic and intimate journalism; (g) writing norms; (h) the performance turn; (i) the performing of ethnography; and (j) the performing of interpretation.

This is a book about how to do interpretive interactionism as a mode of critical qualitative research. Interpretive interactionism attempts to make the meanings that circulate in the world of lived experience accessible to the reader. It endeavors to capture and represent the voices, emotions, and actions of those studied. The focus of interpretive research is on those life experiences that radically alter and shape the meanings persons give to themselves and their experiences.

WHEN TO USE THE
INTERPRETIVE APPROACH

Three questions need to be addressed. First, when should the interpretive approach be used? Second, how can this approach be used to evaluate programs that have been created to deal with "real-life" problems? Third, how do researchers go about doing this kind of research?

Interpretive interactionism is not for everyone. It is based on a research philosophy that is counter to much of the traditional scientific research tradition in the social sciences. Only persons drawn to the qualitative, interpretive approach are likely to use the methods and strategies discussed in this book. Furthermore, I favor an approach that involves minimal theory, seeks to show or perform rather than tell, and is based on a belief that less is more. Writers must be openly present in their texts and must make their values clear.

Not all qualitative researchers will use the methods I propose. *Researchers should use the approach advocated here only when they want to examine the relationships between personal troubles (such as wife battering or alcoholism) and the public policies and public institutions that have been created to address those troubles.* Interpretive interactionism speaks to this interrelationship between private lives and public responses to personal troubles. It works outward from the biography of the person.

At the applied level, the interpretive approach can contribute to evaluative research in the following ways (see Becker, 1967a, p. 23). First, it can help researchers to identify different definitions of the problem and the program being evaluated. It can show, for example, how battered wives interpret the shelters, hot lines, and public services that are made available to them by social welfare agencies. Through the use of personal experience stories and thick descriptions of lived experiences, researchers can compare and contrast the perspectives of clients and workers.

Second, through an interpretive approach, researchers can locate the assumptions that are held by various interested parties—policy makers, clients, welfare workers, on-line professionals—assumptions that are often belied by the facts of experience, and show them to be correct or incorrect (Becker, 1967a, p. 23). Third, researchers can use an interpretive approach to identify strategic points of intervention into social situations. In this way, they can evaluate and improve the services of agencies and programs. Fourth, an interpretive approach makes it possible for researchers to suggest "alternative moral points of view from which the problem," the policy, and the program can be interpreted and assessed (see Becker, 1967a, pp. 23-24). Because of its emphasis on experience and its meanings, the interpretive method suggests that programs must always be judged by and from the point of view of the persons most directly affected. Fifth, researchers can expose the limits of statistics and statistical evaluations by using the more qualitative materials furnished by the interpretive approach. The emphasis of this approach on the uniqueness of each life holds up the individual case as the measure of the effectiveness of all applied programs.

A basic two-part thesis drives the applied focus of this book. As critical theorists, interpretive interactionists are committed to showing how the practices of critical, interpretive qualitative research can help change the world in positive ways. They are committed to creating new ways of making the practices of critical qualitative inquiry central to the workings of a free democratic society. This commitment rests on the importance of interpretation and understanding as key features of social life. In social life there is only interpretation. That is, everyday life revolves around persons' interpreting and making judgments about their own behaviors and experiences and those of others. Many times these interpretations and judgments are based on faulty or incorrect understandings. Individuals, for instance, mistake their own experiences for the experiences of others. They then use these interpretations to formulate social programs that are intended to alter and shape the lives of troubled persons, such as community services for the mentally ill or the homeless, treatment centers for alcoholics, and medical services for AIDS patients.

But often the understandings that these programs are based upon bear little relationship to the meanings, interpretations, and experiences of the persons they are intended to serve. As a consequence, there are gaps or failures in understanding. The programs don't work because they are based on a failure to take into account the perspectives and attitudes of the persons served. The human disciplines and the applied social sciences are under a mandate to clarify how interpretations and understandings are formulated, implemented, and given meaning in problematic, lived situations. Ideally, social scientists can also use this knowledge to evaluate programs that have been put into place to assist troubled persons. *We must grasp, understand, and interpret correctly the perspectives and experiences of those persons who are served by applied programs if we are to create solid and effective programs.* This is the argument that organizes this book.

THE RESEARCHER
AND THE SOCIAL WORLD

The qualitative researcher is not an objective, politically neutral observer who stands outside and above the study of the social world. Rather, the researcher is historically and locally situated within the very processes being studied. A gendered, historical self is brought to this process. This self, as a set of shifting identities, has its own history with the situated practices that define and shape the public issues and private troubles being studied.

In the social sciences today there is no longer a God's-eye view that guarantees absolute methodological certainty. All inquiry reflects the standpoint of the inquirer. All observation is theory-laden. There is no possibility of theory- or value-free knowledge. The days of naive realism and naive positivism are over. In their place stand critical and historical realism as well as various versions of relativism. The criteria for evaluating research are now relative. This is the nonfoundational position.[1]

An antifoundational, critical social science seeks its external grounding not in science, in any of its revisionist, postpositivist forms, but rather in a commitment to a post-Marxism and communitarian feminism with hope but no guarantees. It seeks to understand how power and ideology operate through and across systems of discourse, cultural commodities, and cultural texts. It asks how words, texts, and their meanings play a pivotal part in the culture's "decisive performances of race, class [and] gender" (Downing, 1987, p. 80).

INTERPRETIVE CRITERIA
IN THE SEVENTH MOMENT

In the seventh moment, the criteria for evaluating critical qualitative work are moral and ethical. The following understandings structure this process. First, this is a political, ethical, and aesthetic position. It blends aesthetics, ethics, and epistemologies.[2] It understands that nothing is value-free, that knowledge is power. Further, those who have power determine what is aesthetically pleasing and ethically acceptable. Thus this position erases any distinctions among epistemology, aesthetics, and ethics.

Second, in a feminist, communitarian sense, this aesthetic contends that ways of knowing (epistemology) are moral and ethical (Christians, 2000). These ways of knowing involve conceptions of who the human being is (ontology), including how matters of difference are socially organized. The ways in which these relationships of difference are textually represented answer to a political and epistemological aesthetic that defines what is good, true, and beautiful.

All aesthetics and standards of judgment are based on particular moral standpoints. There is no objective, morally neutral standpoint. Hence, for example, an Afrocentric feminist aesthetic (and epistemology) stresses the importance of truth, knowledge, and beauty ("Black is beautiful"). Such claims are based on a concept of storytelling and a notion of wisdom that is experiential and shared. Wisdom so conceived is derived from local, lived experience and expresses lore, folktale, and myth (Collins, 1990).

Third, this is a dialogical epistemology and aesthetic. It involves a give-and-take and ongoing moral dialogue among persons. It enacts an ethic of care and an ethic of personal and communal responsibility (Collins, 1990, p. 214). Politically, this aesthetic imagines how a truly democratic society might look, including one that is free of race prejudice and oppression. This aesthetic values beauty and artistry, movement, rhythm, color, and texture in everyday life. It celebrates difference and the sounds of many different voices. It expresses an ethic of empowerment.

Fourth, this ethic presumes a moral community that is ontologically prior to the person. This community has shared moral values, including the concepts of shared governance, neighborliness, love, kindness, and the moral good (Christians, 2000, pp. 144-149). This ethic embodies a sacred, existential epistemology that locates persons in a noncompetitive, nonhierarchical relationship to the larger moral universe. This ethic declares that all persons deserve dignity and a sacred status in the world. It stresses the value of human life, truth telling, and nonviolence (Christians, 2000, p. 147).

Fifth, this aesthetic enables social criticism and engenders resistance (see below). It helps persons imagine how things could be different. It imagines new forms of human transformation and emancipation. It enacts these transformations through dialogue. If necessary, it sanctions nonviolent forms of civil disobedience (Christians, 2000, p. 148).

Sixth, this aesthetic understands that moral criteria are always fitted to the contingencies of concrete circumstances, assessed in terms of those local understandings that flow from a feminist, communitarian moral (Christians, 2000). This ethic calls for dialogical research rooted in the concepts of care and shared governance. How this ethic works in any specific situation cannot be known in advance.

Seventh, properly conceptualized, interpretive research becomes a civic, participatory, collaborative project, a project that joins the researcher with the researched in an ongoing moral dialogue. This is a form of participatory action research. It has roots in liberation theology, neo-Marxist approaches to community development, and human rights activism in Asia and elsewhere (Kemmis & McTaggart, 2000, p. 568). Such work is characterized by shared ownership of the research project, community-based analyses, and an emancipatory, dialectical, and transformative commitment to community action (Kemmis & McTaggart, 2000, pp. 568, 598). This form of qualitative research "aims to help people recover, and release themselves, from the constraints embedded in the *social media*" (Kemmis & McTaggart, 2000, p. 598). This means that the researcher learns to take on the identities of advocate and cultural critic (see Ryan, Greene, Lincoln, Mathison, & Mertens, 1998).

Accordingly, eighth, this ethic asks that interpretive work provide the foundations for social criticism and social action. These texts represent calls to action. As a cultural critic, the researcher speaks from an informed moral and ethical position. He or she is anchored in a specific community of moral discourse. The moral ethnographer takes sides.

Moral Criticism and Taking Sides

Taking sides, as indicated above, is a complex process involving several steps (Becker, 1967b). First, researchers must make their own value positions clear, including the so-called objective facts and ideological assumptions that they attach to these positions. Second, they identify and analyze the values and claims to objective knowledge that organize positions that are contrary to their own. Third, they show how these appeals to ideology and objective knowledge reflect particular moral and historical standpoints. Fourth, they show how these standpoints disadvantage and disempower members of a specific group.

Fifth, researchers make an appeal to a participatory, feminist, communitarian ethic. This ethic may represent new conceptions of care, love, beauty, and empowerment. Sixth, they apply this ethic to the specifics of a concrete case, showing how it would and could produce social betterment. Advocates of the black arts movement in the 1970s, for example, asked how much more beautiful a poem, melody, play, novel, or film made the life of a single black person (Gayle, 1971/1997, p. 1876).

Seventh, in a call to action, researchers engage in concrete steps that will change situations in the future. They may teach persons how to bring new value and meaning to identities, cultural commodities, and texts that are marginalized and stigmatized by the larger culture. They demonstrate how particular definitions and meanings negatively affect the lives of specific persons. They indicate how particular texts directly and indirectly misrepresent persons and reproduce prejudice and stereotypes.

Eighth, in advancing this utopian project, critical interpretive researchers seek new standards and new tools of evaluation. For example, Karenga (1972/1997), a theorist of the black arts movement in the 1970s, argued at the time that there were three criteria for black art. Such art, he said, must be functional, collective, and committed. Functionally, this art would support and "respond positively to the reality of a revolution" (p. 1973). It would not be art for art's sake; rather, it would be art for "our sake," art for "Sammy the shoeshine boy, T. C. the truck driver and K. P. the unwilling soldier" (p. 1974). Karenga told blacks, "We do not need pictures of oranges in a bowl, or trees standing innocently in the midst of a wasteland . . . or fat white women smiling lewdly. . . . If we must paint oranges or trees, let our guerrillas be eating those oranges for strength and using those trees for cover" (p. 1974; see also Gayle, 1971/1997).

According to Karenga (1972/1997), collectively, black art comes from people and must be returned to the people "in a form more beautiful and colorful than it was in real life. . . . art is everyday life given more form and color" (p. 1974). Such art is committed, it is democratic, it celebrates diversity as well as personal and collective freedom. It is not elitist.

Blurring Interpretive Genres

The seventh moment is characterized by a willingness to experiment with new representational forms. As interpretive interactionists engage experimental writing forms, a parallel movement is occurring in journalism, and there is much to be learned from these developments. Building on earlier calls for a new journalism (Wolfe, 1973), a current generation of journalists (Harrington, 1997a, 1997b; Kramer, 1995; Sims, 1995) is producing a new writing genre variously termed *literary, intimate,* and *creative nonfiction journalism* (Harrington, 1997a, p. xv). This intimate journalism extends the project of the new journalism of the 1970s, which was based on seven understandings. The new writers of Tom Wolfe's generation treated facts as social constructions; blurred writing genres, combining literary and investigative journalism with the realist novel, the confession, the travel report, and the autobiography; used the scenic method to show rather than tell; wrote about real people and created composite characters; used multiple points of view, including third-person narration, to establish authorial presence; deployed multiple narrative strategies (flashbacks, foreshadowing, interior monologues, parallel plots) to build dramatic tension; and positioned themselves as moral witnesses to the radical changes taking place in American society (Denzin, 1997, p. 131). These writers understood that social life and reports about it were social constructions. Journalists did not map, or report on, objective reality.

I have no desire to reproduce arguments concerning the importance of maintaining some distinction between fictional (literary) and nonfictional (journalism, ethnography) texts. Nor do I distinguish among literary, nonliterary, fictional, and nonfictional textual forms. These are socially and politically constructed categories. They are too often used to police certain transgressive writing forms, such as fictional ethnographies. There is only narrative—that is, only different genre-defined ways of representing and writing about experiences and their multiple realities. The discourses of the postmodern world constantly intermingle literary, poetic, journalistic, fictional, cinematic, documentary, factual, and ethnographic writing and representation. No form is privileged over others; all simply perform different functions for a writer and an interpretive community.

The practices and understandings described above shape the work of the intimate journalists. Writers such as Harrington (1992) use the methods of descriptive realism to produce in-depth, narrative accounts of everyday life, lived up close. They use real-life dialogue, intimate first- and third-person voice, multiple points of view, interior monologues, scene-by-scene narration, and a plain, spare style (Harrington, 1997b, pp. xlii-xlv; Kramer, 1995, p. 24). The writer may be invisible in the text or present as narrator and participant. Here is Harrington (1992) talking about himself; the story is "Family Portrait in Black and White":

> My journey begins in the dentist's chair. The nurse . . . and the doctor are [telling] funny stories about their kids, when in walks another dentist. . . . "I've got a good one," he says cheerfully, and then he tells a racist joke. I can't recall the joke, only that it ends with a black man who is stupid. Dead silence. It's just us white folks here in the room, but my dentist and his nurse know my wife, who is black, and they know my son and daughter, who are, as they describe themselves, tan and bright tan. How many racist jokes have I heard in my life? . . . for the first time . . . I am struck with a deep sharp pain. I look at this man, with his pasty face, pale hair and weak lips, and I think: This idiot is talking about my children! (p. 1)

Compare this telling, with its first-person narration, to Leon Dash's (1997) description of Rosa Lee:

> Rosa Lee Cunningham is thankful that she doesn't have to get up early this morning. She is dozing, floating back and forth between sleep and drowsiness. Occasionally she hears the muted conversations of the nurses and doctors puttering around the nurse's station. . . . She's tired and worn down. . . . A full night's sleep and daylong quiet are rare luxuries in her life. This is the closest she ever comes to having a vacation. . . . Rosa Lee . . . is fifty-two years old, a longtime heroin addict . . . a member of the urban underclass. . . . [She] has no intention of ending her heroin use. (p. 3)

Harrington speaks only for himself. He is fully present in his text. Dash is invisible. He is the all-knowing observer. He is the fly on the wall narrating an unfolding scene. Dash describes a world, whereas Harrington talks about how it feels to be present in a world. Each writer creates a scene. Each penetrates the images that surround a situation. Harrington and Dash both use sparse, clean prose. Each creates a vivid image of his subject, Harrington of himself, Dash of Rosa Lee. On the other hand, Dash presumes to know what Rosa Lee is feeling and thinking. Hers is a story waiting to be told, and he will tell it. In contrast, Harrington's text suggests that stories are not waiting to be told; rather, they are constructed by the writer, who attempts to impose order on some set of experiences or perceived events.

Both writers ground their prose in facts and their meanings. Dash, however, works with so-called verifiable, factually accurate facts, whereas

Harrington writes of impressions and truths that, although not necessarily factually accurate, are aesthetically and emotionally true. If something did not happen, it could have happened, and it will happen in Harrington's text. Accounts like Harrington's and Dash's invoke the felt life. The goal of such writers is to understand "other people's worlds from the inside out, to understand and portray people as they understand themselves" (Harrington, 1997b, p. xxv). The intent is to build an emotional relationship joining the writer, the life told about, and the reader.

A year later, Harrington (1992) returns to his experience in the dentist's chair:

> What I discovered while waiting in the dentist's chair more than a year ago . . . still remains the greatest insight I have to share: *The idiot was talking about my kids!*
>
> I remember a time when my son was a baby. It was late at night . . . I sat in the dark of my son's room. . . . I watched his face grimace . . . in the shadows. And then, in time so short it passed only in the mind, my son was gone and I was the boy . . . and my father was me. . . . just as suddenly, I was gone again and the light was falling across the knees of my son, who was grown, who was a father, who was me. . . . this kind of understanding changes everything. Only when I *became* black by proxy—through my son, through my daughter—could I see the racism I had been willing to tolerate. Becoming black, even for a fraction of an instant, created an urgency for justice that I couldn't feel as only a white man, no matter how good-hearted. . . . no white man in his or her right mind would yet volunteer to trade places, become black, in America today. (p. 447)

Such writing connects readers to their newspapers by producing narratives about people in extreme and ordinary situations. These stories, or journalistic case studies, politicize the everyday world, illuminating the structures and processes that shape individuals' lives and their relations with others. In so doing, they "nurture civic transformation" (Harrington, 1997a, p. xiv; see also Harrington, 1997b, p. xviii).[3]

Civic Transformations

At the moment of civic transformation, intimate journalism joins with the call for public journalism, a critical ethnographic journalism that fuses persons and their troubles with public issues and the public arena. This is interpretive interactionism with another name. A pragmatic, civic journalism invites readers to become participants, not mere spectators, in the public dramas that define meaningful, engaged life in society today. Public journalism creates the space for local ethnographies of problematic community and personal experiences. This is a socially responsible civic journalism. It advocates participatory democracy. It gives a public voice to the biographically meaningful, epiphanic experiences that occur within the confines of the local moral community.[4] This form of journalistic ethnography speaks to the morally committed reader. This is a reader who is a coparticipant in a public project that demands democratic solutions to personal and public problems (Charity, 1995, p. 146; Rosen, 1994).[5]

Taken to the next level, transformed into public-journalism-as-ethnography, this writing answers to the following goals. Critical, intimate, public ethnography does the following things:

- It presents the public with in-depth, intimate stories of problematic everyday life, lived up close. These stories create moral compassion and help citizens make intelligent decisions and take public action on private troubles that have become public issues, including helping to get these action proposals carried out (Charity, 1995, p. 2; Mills, 1959, p. 8).

- It promotes interpretive works that raise public and private consciousness. These works help persons collectively to work through the decision-making process. They help isolate choices and core values, utilize expert and local systems of knowledge, and facilitate deliberative, civic discourse (Charity, 1995, pp. 4-8).

- It rejects the classic model of investigative journalism, where the reporter exposes corruption, goes on crusades, roots "out the inside story, tells the brave truth, faces down the Joseph McCarthys and Richard Nixons . . . comforts the afflicted and afflicts the comfortable" (Charity, 1995, p. 9).

- It seeks the ethnographer and journalist who is an expert on the history and public life of the local community, who knows how to listen to and talk to citizens, and how to hear and present consensus when it emerges, and who is also a full-time citizen and committed to the belief that public life can be made to work (Charity, 1995, p. 10).

- It sees the writer as a watchdog for the local community, a person who writes stories that contribute to deliberative, participatory discourse, thereby maintaining the public's awareness of its own voice (Charity, 1995, pp. 104-105, 127).

- It values writing that moves a public to meaningful judgment and meaningful action (Charity, 1995, p. 50). A central goal is civic transformation (Christians, Ferre, & Fackler, 1993, p. 14).

- It exposes complacency, bigotry, and wishful thinking (Charity, 1995, p. 146) while "attempting to strengthen the political community's capacity to understand itself, converse well, and make choices" (Rosen, 1994, p. 381).

- It seeks dramatic stories, narratives that separate facts from stories, telling moving accounts that join private troubles with public issues (Charity, 1995, p. 72; Mills, 1959, p. 8).

- It promotes a form of textuality that turns citizens into readers and readers into persons who take democratic action in the world (Charity, 1995, pp. 19, 83-84).

These are goals, ideals, ways of merging critical interactionism with applied action research, with the new public journalism, and with qualitative research in the seventh moment.

These goals assume a researcher/ethnographer who functions and writes like a literary and intimate public journalist. This means that ethnography as a performer-centered form of storytelling will be given greater emphasis (Degh, 1995, p. 8). A shared public consciousness is sought, a common awareness of troubles that have become issues in the public arena. This consciousness is shaped by a form of writing that merges the personal, the biographical, with the public.

Writing Norms

A feminist, communitarian ethical model produces a series of norms for the public ethnographic writing project.[6] These norms build on and elaborate the four nonnegotiable journalistic norms of accuracy, nonmaleficence, the right to know, and making one's moral position public.[7] The ethnographer's moral tales are not written to produce harm for those who have been oppressed by the culture's systems of domination and repression (the principle of nonmaleficence). The identities of those written about should always be protected. These tales are factually and fictionally correct. When fiction, or imaginative narrative, is written, or when composite cases are molded into a single story, the writer is under an obligation to report this to the reader (see Christians et al., 1993, p. 55).

The reader has the right to read what the ethnographer has learned, but the right to know should be balanced against the principle of nonmaleficence. Accounts should exhibit "interpretive sufficiency" (Christians et al., 1993, p. 120); that is, they should possess depth, detail, emotionality, nuance, and coherence. These qualities assist the reader in forming a critical interpretive consciousness. Such texts should also exhibit representational adequacy, including the absence of racial, class, and gender stereotyping.[8]

The writer must be honest with the reader.[9] The text must be realistic, concrete as to character, setting, atmosphere, and dialogue. The text should provide a forum for the search for moral truths about the self. This forum may explore the unpresentable in the culture; the discontents and violence of contemporary life are documented and placed in narrative form. This writer stirs up the world, and the writer's story (mystory) becomes part of the tale that is told. The writer has a theory about how the world works, and this theory is never far from the surface of the text. Self-reflexive readers are presumed—readers who seek honest but reflexive works that draw them into the many experiences of daily life.

There remains the struggle to find a narrative voice that writes against a long tradition that favors autobiography and lived experience as the sites for reflexivity and selfhood (Clough, 1994, p. 157). This form of subjective reflexivity can be a trap. It too easily reproduces sad, celebratory, and melo-dramatic conceptions of self, agency, gender, desire, and sexuality. There is a pressing need to invent a reflexive form of writing that turns ethnography and experimental literary texts back "onto each other" (Clough, 1994, p. 162; 1998, p. 134).

Always a skeptic, this new writer is suspicious of conspiracies, align-ments of power and desire that turn segments of the public into victims. So these works trouble traditional, realist notions of truth and verification, ask-ing always who stands to benefit from a particular version of the truth. The intimate journalist as public ethnographer enacts an ethics of practice that privileges the client-public relationship. The ethnographer is a moral advo-cate for the public, although their own personal moral codes may lead indi-vidual researchers to work against the so-called best interests of their clients or particular segments of the public.

The ethnographer's tale is always allegorical, a symbolic tale, a parable that is not just a record of human experience. This tale is a means of experi-ence, a method of empowerment for the reader. It is a vehicle through which readers may discover moral truths about themselves. More deeply, the tale is a utopian story of self and social redemption, a tale that brings a moral compass back into the reader's (and the writer's) life. The ethnographer dis-covers the multiple "truths" that operate in the social world, the stories peo-ple tell one another about the things that matter to them. The intimate jour-nalist writes stories that stimulate critical public discourse. Thus these stories enable transformations in the public and private spheres of everyday life.

PERFORMING ETHNOGRAPHY

I turn next to the concept of the performance text (Conquergood, 1998; Turner, 1986a), illustrating my arguments with materials drawn from an ongoing interpretive ethnography of a small Montana town (Denzin, 1999b, 2000a, 2000b).[10] I seek a set of writing practices that turn notes from the field into texts that are performed. A single, yet complex thesis organizes my argument.

We inhabit a performance-based, dramaturgical culture. The dividing line between performer and audience blurs, and culture itself becomes a dramatic performance. Performance ethnography enters a gendered culture with nearly invisible boundaries separating everyday theatrical performances from formal theater, dance, music, MTV, video, and film (Birringer, 1991, p. 182; Butler, 1990, p. 25; 1997, p. 159; 1999, p. 19). But the matter goes even deeper than blurred boundaries. The performance has become reality. Of this, speaking of gender and personal identity, Butler (1990) is certain. Gender is performative, gender is always doing, "though not a doing by a subject who might be said to preexist the deed. . . . there is no being behind doing. . . . the deed is everything. . . . there is no gender identity behind the expressions of gender. . . . identity is performatively constituted by the very 'expressions' that are said to be its results" (p. 25). Further, the linguistic act is performative, and words can hurt (Butler, 1997, p. 4).

Performance texts are situated in complex systems of discourse, where traditional, everyday, and avant-garde meanings of theater, film, video, ethnography, cinema, performance, text, and audience all circulate and inform one another. As Collins (1990, p. 210) has suggested, the meanings of lived experience are inscribed and made visible in these performances.

Anna Deavere Smith's *Fires in the Mirror* (1993) is an example. In this play, Smith offers a series of performance pieces based on interviews with people involved in a racial conflict in Crown Heights, Brooklyn, on August 19, 1991. The conflict was set in motion when a young black Guyanese boy, Gavin Cato, was accidentally killed by an auto in a police-escorted entourage carrying Lubavitcher Grand Rebbe Menachem Schneerson. Later that day, a group of black men fatally stabbed Yankel Rosenbaum, a 29-year-old Hasidic scholar from Australia. This killing was followed by a racial conflict that lasted 3 days and involved many members of the community. Smith's play has speaking parts for gang members, police officers, anonymous young girls and boys, mothers, fathers, rabbis, the Reverend Al Sharpton, playwright Ntozake Shange, and African American cultural critic Angela Davis.

Cornel West (1993) observes that *Fires in the Mirror* is a "grand example of how art can constitute a public space that is perceived by people as empowering rather than disempowering" (p. xix). Thus blacks, gang members, the police, and the Jewish community all come together and talk in this play. The drama crosses racial boundaries. Smith's text shows that "American character lives not on one place or the other, but in the gaps between places, and in our struggle to be together in our differences" (p. xii).

An Anonymous Young Man #1 Wa Wa Wa, a Caribbean American with dreadlocks, describes the auto accident:

> What I saw was
> she was pushin'
> her brother on the bike like
> this,
> right?
> She was pushin'
> him
> and he keep dippin' around
> like he didn't know how
> to ride the bike . . .
> So she was already runnin'
> when the car was comin' . . .
> we was watchin' the car
> weavin',
> and we was goin'
> "Oh, yo
> it's a Jew man.
> He broke the stop light, they never get arrested."

(A. Smith, 1993, pp. 79-80)

And so in performing this young man's words, Smith contextualizes this drama, showing how it looked from the standpoint of a person who watched the accident unfold.

Performance ethnography simultaneously creates and enacts moral texts, texts that move from the personal to the political, the local to the historical and the cultural. Following Conquergood (1985), these dialogical works create spaces for give-and-take, doing more than turning the other into the object of a voyeuristic, fetishistic, custodial, or paternalistic gaze.

Texts turned into radical street performances act to question and "re-envision ingrained social arrangements of power" (Cohen-Cruz, 1998, p. 1). Such works, in the forms of rallies, puppet shows, marches, vigils, choruses, clown shows, and ritual performances, transport spectators and performers out of everyday reality into idealized spaces where the taken for granted is contested (Cohen-Cruz, 1998, p. 3). Street, or public place, performances offer members of the culture alternative scripts or ways of acting in and hence of changing the world (Cohen-Cruz, 1998, p. 1). Cohen-Cruz (1998, p. 5) suggests that these performances can take several overlapping forms, including *agitprop,* or attempts to mobilize people around a partisan view; *witnessing,* or making a spectacle out of an act that perhaps cannot be changed; *confrontation,* or inserting a performance into people's everyday life, thereby asking them to confront a scenario that is otherwise distant; *utopia,* or enacting an idealized version of reality; and *tradition,* that is, honoring a set of culturally shared beliefs, as in Fourth of July parades in small-town America.

In my performance project I seek minimalist social science, one that uses few concepts. This is a dramaturgical (Branaman, 1997, p. xlix; Goffman, 1959; Lemert, 1997, p. xxiv) or performative anthropology (Jackson, 1998; Turner, 1986) that attempts to stay close to how people represent everyday life experiences. A performative ethnography simultaneously writes and studies performances, showing how people enact cultural meanings in their daily lives.

Shaped by the sociological imagination (Mills, 1959), this version of qualitative inquiry attempts to show how terms such as *biography, gender, race, ethnicity, family,* and *history* interact and shape one another in concrete social situations. These works are usually written in the first-person voice, from the point of view of the sociologist doing the observing and the writing. A minimalist, performative social science is also about stories, performances, and storytelling. When performed well, these stories create a ritual space "where people gather to listen, to experience, to better understand the world and their place in it" (Jenkins, 1999, p. 19).

THE PERFORMANCE TURN

The performance turn in the human disciplines (Conquergood, 1998; Madison, 1999; Phelan & Lane, 1998) poses three closely interrelated problems for a critical, interdisciplinary interpretive project; namely, how to construct, perform, and critically analyze performance texts. Glossing the issues involved in construction and critical analysis, I will privilege performance and coperformance (audience-performer) texts in contrast to single-performer, text-centered approaches to interpretation (see Denzin, 1997, p. 96). Through the act of coparticipation, these works bring audiences back into the text, creating a field of shared emotional experience. The phenomenon being described is created through the act of representation. A resistance model of textual performance and interpretation is foregrounded. A good performance text must be more than cathartic, it must be political, moving people to action, reflection.

The attention to performance is interdisciplinary; sociologists (Kotarba, 1998; Richardson, 1997), anthropologists (Jackson, 1998; Turner, 1986a), communication scholars (Conquergood, 1998), and education theorists (Lather & Smithies, 1997) are calling for texts that move beyond the purely representational and toward the presentational. At the same time, action (Stringer, 1996), communitarian (Christians et al., 1993), feminist (Lather, 1991), constructivist (Lincoln, 1997), cooperative inquiry (Reason, 1993, 1994), and participant researchers (Carspecken, 1996) are exploring non-traditional presentational performance formats. Such works allow community researchers and community members to co-construct meaning through action-based performance projects (Conquergood, 1998). This call merges a feminist, communitarian ethic with a moral ethnography that presumes a researcher who builds collaborative, reciprocal, trusting, friendly relations with those studied.

Performance Texts

Performed texts "have narrators, drama, action, shifting points of view . . . [and] make experience concrete, anchoring it in the here and now" (Paget, 1993, p. 27; see also Mienczakowski, 1995). Centered in the audience-researcher nexus, these texts are the site for "mystories" (Ulmer, 1989)—that is, reflexive, critical stories that feel the sting of memory, stories that enact liminal experiences. These are storied retellings that seek the truth of life's fictions via evocation rather than explanation or analysis. In them, ethnographers, audiences, and performers meet in a shared field of experience, emotion, and action.

Such performances return to memory, not lived experience, as the site of criticism, interpretation, and action. It is understood that experience exists only in its representation; it does not stand outside memory or perception. The meanings of facts are always reconstituted in the telling, as they are remembered and connected to other events. Hence the appeal of the performance text does not lie in its offer of the certainty of the factual. The appeal is more complicated than that. Working from the site of memory, the reflexive, performed text asks readers as viewers (or coperformers) to relive the experience through the writer's or performer's eyes. Readers thus move through the re-created experience with the performer. This allows them to relive the experience for themselves.

Thus we can share in Harrington's experiences when he tells us about remembering the night he held his young son in his arms. The writer acting in this manner re-creates in the mind's eye a series of emotional moments. Life is then retraced through that moment, interpreting the past from the point of view of the present. Here is Susan Krieger (1996):

I have just come back from a trip to Florida to settle the affairs of my lover's aunt [Maxine], who died suddenly at the age of seventy. She was carrying her groceries up the stairs to her apartment when she dropped dead of a heart attack. . . .
. . . It was an otherworldly experience: going to Florida . . . to clean out the house of a woman I did not know—sorting through her clothes and jewelry, finding snapshots she recently took, using her bathroom, meeting her friends. (pp. 65, 68)

On her last day in Florida, Krieger finds Aunt Maxine's silver flatware inside an old accordion case in the back corner of a greasy kitchen cabinet. Maxine's silver is cheap. It had been a replacement set. It is tarnished, not the real thing like the family silver her mother had gotten from her mother. Krieger asks, "What determines the value of a person's life, is value different if you are a woman, how do you separate a woman from the things she owns, leaves behind, her clothes, the cheap family silver?" (p. 70). This cheap set of silver flatware is not an adequate measure of Aunt Maxine.

Laurel Richardson's mother died of breast cancer in Miami Beach on June 8, 1968. Nearly 30 years later, Richardson (1997) wrote about her mother's death:

On June 8, I awoke determined to drive to Key West for the day. I sponge-bathed Mother, greeted the nurse, kissed my parents good-bye, and drove off in Father's Dodge Dart. When I got to Long Key, I was overwhelmed with the need to phone my parents. Mother had just died—less than a minute ago—Father said. (p. 234)

Of this news she observes, "I was grateful to have not witnessed her passing-on. I was thirty years old" (p. 235).

Ten years after her mother's death, Richardson wrote a poem, "Last Conversation" (1997, p. 234):

I want to hold your
weightless body to my

breasts, cradle you,
rock you to sleep.

The truth of a person's and a culture's ways are given in texts like these. Such works, when performed or read, become symbolic representations of what the culture and the person values. In their performances, performers embody these values.

Now listen to Angela Davis. In her recent study of the female blues singers Ma Rainey, Bessie Smith, and Billie Holiday, Davis (1998) observes that within African American culture the "blues marked the advent of a popular culture of performance, with the borders of performer and audience becoming increasing differentiated. . . . this . . . mode of presenting popular music crystallized into a performance culture that has had an enduring influence on African-American music" (p. 5).

In their performances, Ma Rainey, Bessie Smith, and Billie Holiday presented a set of black feminist understandings concerning class, race, gender, violence, sexuality, marriage, men, and intimacy (Collins, 1990, p. 209). This blues legacy is deeply entrenched in an indigenous, class-conscious, black feminism. The female blues singers created performance spaces for black women, spaces to sing and live the blues, black female voices talking about and doing black culture onstage, a public, critical performance art (see Jones, 1999).

The blues are improvised songs sung from the heart about love and about women and men gone wrong (Collins, 1990, p. 210). Rainey, Smith, and Holiday sang in ways that went beyond the written text. They turned the blues into a living art form, a form that would, with Holiday, move into the spaces of jazz. And jazz, like the blues and culture, is an improvisational, not static, art form. Bill Evans, the great bebop pianist, put it this way, "Jazz is not a what . . . it is a how. If it were a what, it would be static, never growing. The how is that the music comes from the moment, it is spontaneous, it exists at the time it is created" (quoted in Lees, 1996, p. 426). The improvised coperformance text, the jazz solo, like Billie Holiday singing the blues, is a spontaneous production; it lives in the moment of creation. The how of culture as it connects people to one another in loving, conflictual, and disempowering ways is what performance ethnography seeks to capture (see Jackson, 1998, p. 21).

Narrative Collage, Performance Writing, and Performance Texts

Performance texts build on narrative collage, which is the shattering of narrative line. Dillard (1982) compares narrative collage to cubism:

> Just as Cubism can take a roomful of furniture and iron it into nine square feet of canvas, so fiction can take fifty years of human life, chop it to bits and piece these bits together so that, within the limits of the temporal form, we can consider them all at once. This is narrative collage. (p. 21)

In the performance text, storied sequences do not necessarily follow a progression. Narrative collage fractures time; speakers leap forward and backward in time. Time is not attached to causal sequences, to "fixed landmarks in orderly progression" (Dillard, 1982, p. 21). Time, space, and character are flattened out. The intervals between temporal moments can be collapsed in an instant. More than one voice can speak at once, in more than one tense. The text can be a collage, a montage, with photographs, blank spaces, poems, monologues, dialogues, voice-overs, and interior streams of consciousness.

The performance text, as shown in the excerpts above, engages in a form of performance writing (Pollock, 1998; see also Phelan, 1998, pp. 12-14). Using the methods of narrative collage, performance writing shows, rather than tells. It is writing that speaks performatively, enacting what it describes. It is writing that does what it says it is doing by doing it. Performative writing "is an inquiry into the limits and possibilities of the intersections between speech and writing. . . . [It] evokes what it names" (Phelan, 1998, p. 13). Performative writing is not a matter of formal style per se, nor is it writing that is avant-garde or clever (Pollock, 1998, p. 75). Pollock (1998, pp. 80-95) suggests that performative writing is evocative, reflexive, and multivoiced; it crisscrosses genres and is always partial and incomplete. But in performative writing, things happen; it is writing that is consequential, and it is about a world that is already being performed.

To say that Anna Deavere Smith writes performatively is to say that her scripts allow persons to experience their own subjectivity in the moment of performance. Performance writing is poetic and dramatic. It transforms literal (and transcribed) speech into speech that is first person, active, in motion, processual. In such texts, performance and performativity are intertwined, each defining the other. The performer's performance creates a space the other enters.

Performance texts enact performance writing. They allow experience to come alive, turning it into remembered series of events represented in the form of dialogues, poems, or stories. The subject of the text becomes a performative accomplishment; personal narrative is materialized, or made real, in the act of performance. Performance comes between experience and story. Narrative mediates experience (Langellier, 1999, p. 128). Performance erases the distinction between showing and telling.

After Conquergood (1998), three views of performance can be distinguished: "the movement from performance as *mimesis* to *poiesis* to *kinesis*, performance as imitation, construction, dynamism" (p. 31). The sociologist

Erving Goffman, Conquergood suggests, treats performance as imitation, whereas Victor Turner's (1986a) constructional theory of performance moves from mimesis to poiesis. John Searle's (1969) theory of speech acts, developed by Judith Butler (1990), stresses the performative features of action, utterances that do things in the world, promises, apologies. For Butler, each person constitutes through his or her interactional performances a situated version of a heterosexual or nonheterosexual identity. Every performance is a masquerade, a copy of the real thing, an imitation of an imitation that establishes itself performatively as an original. But this is always a parody, for there is no original, no point where nothing came before.

If there is no original, then the concept of performance as mimesis is a challenge. However, as Taussig (1993) and Haraway (1991, p. 201) show, imitation can be subversive, like the Coyote, "witty actor and agent, the coding trickster with whom we must learn to converse" (Haraway, 1991, p. 201; see also Taussig, 1993, p. 255). So even the imitation is an original. Further, every performance becomes a form of kinesis, or motion. A performance is an instance of a politics of action, a circulation of power. A performance is a decentering of agency and person through movement, disruption, action that incessantly contests, breaks, and remakes (Conquergood, 1998, p. 32). Personal narrative and personhood are constituted in the moments of performance.

Every performance becomes a way of questioning the status quo, a way of transgressing, a force that "crashes and breaks through sedimented meanings and normative traditions and plunges us back into the vortices of political struggle . . . movement beyond boundaries" (Conquergood, 1998, p. 32). And even as performance reproduces the status quo, it does so in novel ways, in ways special to the performer.

RED LODGE, MONTANA:
EXPERIENCES AND PERFORMANCES

William Kittredge (1996, p. 97) says that the West is an enormous empty and innocent stage waiting for a performance (see also Kittredge, 1987, 1994). He continues, "We see the history of our performances everywhere . . . inscribed on the landscape (fences, roads, canals, power lines, city plans, bomb ranges)" (p. 97). Moreover, the West is contained in the stories people tell about it. Montana is both a performance and a place for performances. It is not possible to write an objective, authoritative, neutral account of performing Montana. Every account is personal and locally situated. Here are some of the ways Montana is performed.

In 1994, my wife and I bought a little piece of land outside Red Lodge, Montana, population 1,875.[11] We got an acre with a cabin on a river called Rock Creek and a big bluff of a rock outcropping behind the cabin. Our little valley is marked by lakes, snowcapped mountain ranges, alpine meadows, and sprawling ranches where people live in double-wide mobile homes. Early June brings fields of yellow sunflowers, bright red Indian paintbrush, and soft blue lupine.

In the summer, horses and deer graze in the valley above the road to our cabin. Off the big boulder under the big cottonwood tree, I catch rainbow and brook trout for breakfast. I fish; my wife quilts, hikes, and collects wildflowers. Last Christmas my wife took up cross-country skiing. In the summer we go to auctions and yard sales, and drive into town for groceries.

After reading Kittredge and studying Turner (1986a) and Bruner (1986, 1989, 1996), I have come to see our little part of Montana as a liminal place, a place for new performances, new stories. Caught up in the shadows of the new, mythologized culture of the West (Limerick, 1997, p. 151; Wilkinson, 1997, p. 114), we are learning how to perform Montana. We are learning to engage in the ritual performances that people do when they are in and around Red Lodge, performances such as going to parades, shopping in the little craft and antique stores, buying things for the cabin, driving over the mountain, eating out, having an espresso on the sidewalk in front of the Coffee Factory Roasters, having a fancy dinner at the Pollard (which is on the National Registry of Hotels), picking up pictures from Flash's Image Factory, buying quilting materials at Granny Hugs, and volunteering in the local library, which is computerizing its entire collection.

We watch other people do what we are doing, separating the experience of being in Montana from its performances and representations, constructing culture and meaning as they go along (Bruner, 1989, p. 113). Three years ago, I overheard a man talking to the owner of the tackle shop in Big Timber. His BMW was still running out front, the driver's door open. He had on an Orvis fishing vest. He had driven with his family from Connecticut. "The kids saw that movie *A River Runs Through It*. Where do we have to go to catch fish like they did in that movie? Can somebody around here give me fly-fishing lessons?" The owner said no on the lessons, but told the man to "go about 20 miles upriver, past Four-Mile Bridge. You can't miss it" (see also Dawson, 1996, p. 11).

Of course, the meanings of these Montana performance experiences are constantly changing. It is not appropriate to judge them in terms of their authenticity or originality. There is absolutely no original against which any given performance can be measured. There are only performances that seem to work and those that do not.

Performing Interpretation, Creating Local History

Every year, we try to observe part of Red Lodge's Festival of Nations celebration. This is a 9-day ritual performance that reenacts the town's white European ethnic history. It involves white rituals such as colorful Old World costumes; Finnish, Irish, and Scottish dances and songs; bagpipes and the New Caledonia Drum and Bugle Corps; and cowboy poets—"whiteness as race, as privilege, as social construction" (Fine, Powell, Weis, & Wong, 1997, p. vii). This is whiteness as moral community. The souls of white folk are on public display (Du Bois, 1920, p. 29; Hughes, 1962).

Each day of the festival is given a name—7 days are devoted to specific nationalities (Irish-English-Welsh, German, Scandinavian, Finnish, Italian, Slavic, and Scottish), and the other days are Montana Day and All Nations Day. At the beginning of the 20th century, men from the European countries saluted in the festival came to Montana and became miners. Later they married, and their wives taught school, cooked, had children, helped run little shops, and carried on native crafts from their home countries. Red Lodge tries to keep this history alive.

According to local history, the festival started shortly after World War II. Local community leaders decided to build a civic center. They wanted a place for community activities, for an annual summer music festival, for art and craft exhibits and the display of flags and cultural items from each of the nations represented in the town. Thus was born the Festival of Nations, and Red Lodge was soon transformed into a "tourist town, a place that offered good scenery, fine fishing, the Hi-Road, the rodeo, cool summers" (Red Lodge Chamber of Commerce, 1982, p. 4). But the town had more to offer: "The inhabitants themselves were a resource" (p. 4). For 9 days every summer, Red Lodge puts its version of local ethnic culture on display, turning everyday people into performers of their respective ethnic heritages.

In these performances, residents only had their own histories to go on, so they made it up as they went along, one day for each ethnic group, but each group would do pretty much the same thing: a parade down Broadway with national flags from the country of origin, people in native costume, an afternoon performance of some sort (singing, storytelling, rug making), ethnic food in the Labor Temple (every day from 3:00 to 5:00 p.m.), an evening of music and dance in the civic center. This is improvised ethnicity connected to the performance of made-up rituals handed down from one generation to the next, white privilege, white cultural memory, Montana style (see also Hill, 1997, p. 245).

Montana Jazz

I like Montana Day, especially that part that involves ranch women reading their stories about being Montana wives. This is improvised theater, cowgirl women singing their version of the blues—Montana jazz. A tent is set up over the dance pavilion in Lions Park, just next to the Depot Gallery, which is housed in a converted red train caboose, across the street from the Carnegie Library. White plastic chairs are lined up in rows on the lawn. Loudspeakers are on each side of the stage. An old-fashioned Montana rancher meal is served afterward: barbecued beef, baked beans, coleslaw, baked potatoes, Jell-o salad, brownies for dessert, coffee and iced tea for beverages.

Tall and short middle-aged, suntanned women take the stage. These are hardworking women, mothers, daughters, and grandmothers who live in the ranches in the Beartooth Valley, along the East Rosebud, Rock Creek, Willow Creek, and Stillwater River south of Columbus and Absarokee. Some have on cowboy boots, others wear Nike sneakers. They are dressed in blue jeans and decorated red, white, and blue cowboy shirts and skirts, and have red bandannas around their necks. They have short and long hair, ponytails and curls. They read cowboy poetry, tell short stories about hard winters and horses that freeze to death in snowbanks. Some sing songs. Country music plays quietly, and people come and go, some stopping and listening for a while. As these women perform, old ranchers in wide-brimmed cowboy hats close their eyes and tap their feet to the music. Young children run around through the crowd, and husbands proudly watch their wives read their poetry. Like Ma Rainey, Bessie Smith, and Billie Holiday, these women sing their version of the cowgirl blues. And there is a certain firm truth in the way they do this.

Dead Indians

Fiedler (1988) argues that Montana as a white territory became psychologically possible only after the Native Americans, the Nez Percé, Blackfeet, Sioux, Assinboine, Gros Ventre, Cheyenne, Chipewayan, Cree, and Crow were killed, driven away, or forced onto reservations. He asserts that the struggle to rid the West of the "noble savage" and the "redskin" was integral to the myth of the Montana frontier as a wild wilderness (p. 745). According to Fiedler, the Indian was Montana's Negro, an outcast living in an open-air ghetto (p. 752). With the passing of the Native American came trappers, mountain men, explorers, General Custer, Chief Joseph, and then ranchers and homesteaders. Indian sites were marked with names such as Dead Indian Pass.

Entering Red Lodge, you drive past a wooden statue of a Native American, a male Indian face sitting on a big stone. It was carved by a non-Native American. The history of Montana's relations with the Native American is folded into mountain man festivals and events like Montana Day in Red Lodge. It is a history that simultaneously honors the dead Indian while denying the violent past that is so central to white supremacy.

PERFORMING MONTANA

There are many ways to perform Montana. Montana is a place where locals and tourists constantly commingle, where Orvis-outfitted fly fishermen from Connecticut connect with Huck Finn look-alike local kids who fish with worms and old bamboo poles. These Montana performances mix up many different things at the same time—different identities, different selves: cowboys, rodeos, classical music, antique hunters, skiers, mountain men, Finnish women who make rugs, ranchers' wives who write poetry, men who fish for trout.

Being in nature is a major part of the Montana self. My wife and I enact nature; we bring it to ourselves through the very act of bending down and smelling a wildflower, of walking along the river. This contact with the "natural world is an experience that comes to us like a gift" (Kittredge, 1996, p. 108). And so our corner of Montana is a sacred place, a hole, or house of sky, to use phrases from Kittredge (1994) and Doig (1978), a place where wonderful things happen, and they happen when we perform them.

These are the kinds of things a minimalist, storytelling, performative form of qualitative inquiry makes visible. In these tellings the world comes alive. The qualitative researcher attempts to make these meanings available to the reader, hoping to show how this version of the sociological imagination engages some of the things that matter in everyday life.

NOTES

1. There are three basic positions on the issue of evaluative criteria: foundational, quasi-foundational, and nonfoundational. *Foundationalists* apply the same positivist criteria to qualitative research as are employed in quantitative inquiry, contending that there is nothing about qualitative research that demands a special set of evaluative criteria. *Quasi-foundationalists* contend that a set of criteria unique to qualitative research must be

developed (see Smith & Deemer, 2000). *Nonfoundationalists* reject in advance all epistemological criteria.

2. Some definitions: *Aesthetics* refers to theories of beauty; *ethics* refers to theories of ought, of right, a set of principles; *morality* refers to ways of acting, mores, forms of cultural practice; *epistemology* refers to theories of knowing.

3. The following section draws from Denzin (1997, pp. 280-281).

4. At the same time it is understood that "participating in a citizen's initiative to clean up a polluted harbor is no less political than debating in cultural journals the pejorative presentation of certain groups in terms of stereotypical images" (Benhabib, 1992, p. 104).

5. Public journalism is not without its critics, including those who say it is news by focus group, that it is a marketing device to sell newspapers, that it is a conservative, reform movement aimed at increasing the power of professional journalists, and that its advocates do not understand the real meanings of community, public life, or civic discourse. See the essays in Graber, McQuail, and Norris (1998) and Glasser (1999), but see also Carey (1995).

6. This ethic values community, solidarity, care, love, empowerment, morally involved observers, and caring relations with the community (see Denzin, 1997, p. 275).

7. These are extensions of the norms that Christians et al. (1993, pp. 55-57) see as operating for journalists.

8. I thank Clifford Christians for bringing this principle to my attention.

9. The rules in this paragraph plagiarize Raymond Chandler's "Twelve Notes on the Mystery Story" (1995).

10. The following section draws from and reworks portions of Denzin (1999b).

11. There are various stories about how the town got its name. "The generally accepted theory is that the Crow Indians who inhabited the area colored their lodges with red clay" (Graetz, 1997, p. 23).

2

The Interpretive Point of View

This chapter defines the essential features of interpretive interactionism as a perspective and method. The following topics are discussed: (a) key terms; (b) the epiphany; (c) existential inquiry; (d) naturalism; (e) pure and applied interpretive research; (f) positivism and postpositivism; (g) gender, power, history, emotion, and knowledge; (h) the criteria of interpretation; and (i) the interpretive agenda.

Interpretive interactionists want to interpret, perform, and change the world. They understand that qualitative methods are material and interpretive practices. These practices do not stand outside politics and cultural criticism. Interpretive methodologies advance the project of critically imagining and pursuing a more democratic society. This utopian spirit has been a guiding feature of cultural studies and interpretive interactionism from the very beginning.

The method I develop in this chapter involves the collection, writing, and performance of thickly described personal experience stories. These stories are connected to problematic human interactions. In Chapters 3 through 6, I detail how this process works. It is basically quite simple. The researcher listens to and records the stories persons tell one another, and then supplements these stories by conducting open-ended, creative, active interviewing (Douglas, 1985; Holstein & Gubrium, 1995). Thick descriptions, interpretations, and performance texts are generated out of these stories. There is nothing magical or mysterious about this method. It involves using skills that most individuals already have, namely, the ability to talk and listen to others, including oneself, and remembering what one hears others say.

These texts are written from the site of memory, not experience itself. Here is an example.

PERFORMING RACIAL MEMORIES

On July 28, 1966, Edge City desegregated its 10 elementary schools. The local newspaper said that Edge City was the first town in Illinois to do this (see Denzin, Fields, Feinberg, & Roberts, 1997).

Mrs. Anderson was the only woman on the all-white school board that made the decision to desegregate. I had read stories about her in the paper, seen her picture. I knew that she had been a secretary at one of the grade schools. The newspaper said she died in her home, at 6:35 p.m. on November 10, 1996. She was 81 years old, a victim of old age and emphysema. Toward the end of her life, when I interviewed her in her home, a long, clear-plastic tube connected her to an oxygen tank.[1] She breathed with great effort and had brief spells of intense coughing. She had the look of a patrician, elegant in her velvet floor-length blue robe. She had a commanding presence, tall and graceful, but she was slow in her movements, held back by the hose connecting her to her oxygen. Her chair faced a picture window that looked out into her small, well-cared-for backyard, a fenced garden with roses, bird feeders, evergreens, and a dying river birch.

A jar of jelly beans was on the coffee table next to the sofa where I sat. I put the tape recorder next to Mrs. Anderson's chair and pinned the microphone to the collar of her robe, careful not to disturb the oxygen tube. She began to speak, to tell her story about how desegregation happened in Edge City. Her story moves from the mid-1960s to the present.

> It started with two people,
> James and Marilyn Daniels.
> They led a group of their neighbors
> in the black neighborhood.
> They said:
> Look, you're moving all those kids
> from university housing by bus to school.
> Why don't you take Martin School
> and bring them up here and take
> King school kids out to the various neighborhoods?

Pause.

> And thirty years later
> I look back and wonder
> at what kind of courage it took
> for those people to say that.
> And so after some talking about it back and forth . . .
> we had a six to one vote . . .
> But they came to us.
> I don't think we were actually
> aware of the fact that
> there was a segregated school over there. . . .

I think probably at heart
we didn't know how racist
we were behaving by allowing
the school to stay there.

She coughs. She gets up and goes to the kitchen and gets a glass of water.
She comes back and looks out the window. The phone rings. She ignores it.
She returns to her thoughts:

I remember the night
we voted on it. I remember—
It's stupid,
you remember what you thought,
not what you said.
I said,
Well we're only 12 years late.
Let's go.
And I said
Something
stupid and female,
like
I'd be honored.
I sat there and said to
myself,
This is historic.
We are doing something historic.

Of course this did not happen all at once.
There were community meetings
before the board voted,
one meeting involved the parents from university housing.
We met with people at Martin School.
That was ghastly.
We sat up front.

The board and the people
asked us questions and then they
got a little nasty.

I was not frightened,
but I was so unhappy.

A graduate student
stood up
and said,
Those people
those African
Americans
don't want to leave their homes
and
their schools. . . .

"Those people"
has haunted me for 30 years.

Pause.

We only had one outspoken
racist
on the board
at that time
he is
dead now
and
we can speak ill of the dead.
He happened to be a National
Guard,
that was his
bread and butter.
The night we voted,
he had just come
back
from Chicago
where the Guard had been sent
to hold down some of
the riots.
And he turned to me
and said,
You haven't been in Chicago and
listened to those black bastards
calling you names.

"No" was his vote.

I had a different upbringing than many folks
I guess.
For years
I can remember my mother saying,
The happiest years of my life
were the 10 years we lived next door
to a Negro family down in Joliet.
And I don't know if that impressed me
that Negroes were people
or what,
but I remembered it and felt it
and
I have some black
friends today.

See the picture on the VCR?

I cross the room and remove the large family photo from the top of the VCR and hand it to Mrs. Anderson, who hands it back to me. It is a close-up color photo, a blow-up, showing four people, mother and father in the back and two children, two little girls, in the front. The father is black, the children mulatto, the mother white. Mrs. Anderson explains:

That is my older daughter
and her
husband
and
my two beautiful grandchildren.

Aren't they pretty.

As I prepare to leave Mrs. Anderson's house, I remind her that the newspapers called the summer of 1968 "Edge City's *Summer of Discontent*." She is quick to respond:

They must have taken the Summer of Discontent
from the John Steinbeck novel.
They had to have taken it from
someone.
They were not that clever.

Six days after the interview, Mrs. Anderson calls me at home. It is early evening.

> Hello, Dr. Denzin,
> this is Alice Anderson.
> After you left last week
> I remembered
> I kept a scrapbook of the years
> I was on the school board.
> I think you should have it.
> I want someone
> to tell my story,
> now that I am getting so old.
> You are welcome to it,
> if you want it.

Reading Mrs. Anderson's Performance

I have turned Mrs. Anderson's interview into a dramatic, poetic text. Anna Deavere Smith (1993) says that such texts should evoke the character of the speakers. They should allow the speakers to be fully present in their speech.

Mrs. Anderson uses irony to convey her views of the world, a racist world she disdains. With her words she creates a narrative montage. Inside this world of jumbled images and memories she looks back, locating herself in the summer of 1966. Thirty years after the fact, she sees courage in the actions of James and Marilyn Daniels. She sees that she and her colleagues allowed themselves not to see the segregated school "over there." And she applies the term *racist* to this gaze. But she says that when she voted, she voted as a woman.

In her montage, Mrs. Anderson separates herself from other white people. Her family lived next door to a Negro family in Joliet, and she came to see that Negroes were people too. She passed this understanding along to her daughter, as the family photo dramatically demonstrates.

All did not go well in Edge City's desegregation experiment. The summer of 1966 was one of discontent. In her obituary there is no mention of Mrs. Anderson's part in this history. The newspaper does not even record the fact that she served on the school board.

PERSONAL BIOGRAPHY

Interpretive research begins and ends with the biography and the self of the researcher. The events and troubles the researcher writes about are those that he or she has experienced or witnessed firsthand. As David Sudnow (1979) argues, the individual's perspective is "definitionally critical for establishing the 'what' " (p. 154) and, I would add, the "how" of problematic social experience. The task is to produce "richly detailed" descriptions and accounts of such experiences (Sudnow, 1979, p. 154). In this project the writer has "no body but himself to consult" (Sudnow, 1979, p. 154). Important consequences follow from this position: Only you can write your experiences. No one else can write them for you. No one else can write them better than you can. What you write is important.

Clarifying Terms

Before I go on with this discussion, a number of terms need to be defined:

- *Interpretive:* Explaining the meaning of; interpreting, or conferring meaning.
- *Interpreter:* One who interprets, or translates, meaning for others.
- *Interaction:* Action between individuals; the capability of mutual action that is emergent. For human beings, interaction is symbolic, involving the use of language—hence the term *symbolic interaction.*
- *Problematic interaction:* Interactional sequences that give primary meaning to subjects' lives. Such experiences alter how individuals define themselves and their relations with others. In these moments individuals reveal personal character.
- *Interpretive interactionism:* The point of view that confers meaning on problematic symbolic interaction.

Interpretive interactionists are interpreters of problematic, lived experiences involving symbolic interaction between two or more persons.

An Exemplar

Consider the following excerpt from Dostoyevsky's (1866/1950) description of the murder committed by Raskolnikov in *Crime and Punishment:*

> His hands were fearfully weak, he felt them every moment growing more numb and more wooden. He was afraid he would let the axe slip and fall. . . .
> A sudden giddiness came over him. . . . He had not a minute more to lose.

He pulled the axe quite out, swung it with both arms, scarcely conscious of himself, and almost without effort, almost mechanically, brought the blunt side down on her head. . . . The old woman was . . . so short, the blow fell on top of her skull. She cried out, but very faintly . . . he dealt her another blow. . . . the blood gushed as from an overturned glass. . . . He stepped back . . . trying all the time not to get smeared by the blood. (p. 71)

In this account, which is rich in descriptive detail, Dostoyevsky brings alive the moment of Raskolnikov's crime. He describes Raskolnikov's thoughts and feelings as he acted. He describes the act in detail. He brings the reader into the situation. The remainder of the novel deals with the meanings of this crime for Raskolnikov. Interpretive interactionists seek to produce, perform, and interpret records like this.

THE INTERPRETIVE HERITAGE

The critical interpretive approach followed in this book is associated with the works of a number of different scholars, including Marx, Mead, James, Peirce, Dewey, Heidegger, Gadamer, Gramsci, Weber, Husserl, Sartre, Scheler, Merleau-Ponty, Schutz, Barthes, Derrida, Lacan, Geertz, Haraway, Hill-Collins, Anzaldúa, hooks, Trinh, Rosaldo, Smith, Habermas, Hall, Blumer, Becker, Goffman, Garfinkel, and Strauss. It is present in a variety of disciplines—communication, education, history, anthropology, psychology, sociology, political science, business, health and medicine, social work, English and comparative literature, and philosophy, to list a few.

It goes by a variety of names, including interpretive anthropology or sociology, hermeneutics, cultural studies, phenomenology, symbolic interactionism, ethnomethodology, the case study method, and Chicago school sociology. Yet it would be a mistake to categorize all of these approaches under the single label of *interpretive*. There are as many differing interpretive perspectives in the social sciences as there are practitioners who utilize the critical, qualitative, naturalistic, literary methodology that defines the approach.

Some aim for grounded theory. Others seek out generic processes and concepts. Some impose a grand theoretical structure upon the interpretive enterprise, seeking a totalizing theory of human societies, human actions, and human history. Still others formulate ideal types and assess their theory-interpretive work in terms of such concepts as empirical adequacy and empirical validity. Some eschew such subjective concepts as self, intention, meaning, and motive and search only for invariant, publicly observable patterns of action. They seek to locate these patterns in the taken-for-granted structures of the everyday world of conversation and interaction.

A book could be written on these several varieties of the interpretive approach in the human disciplines. For obvious reasons, I have chosen not to write such a book. I offer, instead, my version of interpretation and give it the name *interpretive interactionism.* This phrase signifies an attempt to join the traditional symbolic interactionist approach with the interpretive, phenomenological works of Heidegger and the tradition associated with hermeneutics. Interpretive interactionism also draws upon recent work in feminist social theory, postmodern theory, and the critical-biographical method formulated by C. Wright Mills, Jean-Paul Sartre, and Maurice Merleau-Ponty. It aims to construct studies, performances, and texts that make sense of and criticize the postmodern period of human experience (Baudrillard, 1983; Lyotard, 1984; Mills, 1959).

OPENING UP THE
WORLD FOR INTERPRETATION

As a distinctly qualitative approach to social research, interpretive interactionism attempts to make the world of lived experience visible to the reader. As indicated above, the focus of interpretive research is on those life experiences that radically alter and shape the meanings persons give to themselves and their life projects. This existential thrust (Sartre, 1943/1956) sets this research apart from other interpretive approaches that examine the more mundane, taken-for-granted properties and features of everyday life (Douglas & Johnson, 1977, pp. vii-xv; Garfinkel, 1967; Goffman, 1974; Johnson, 1977). It leads to a focus on the "epiphany."

THE SUBJECT'S EXPERIENCES
AND THE EPIPHANY

Those interactional moments that leave marks on people's lives, like the murder described by Dostoyevsky or Mrs. Anderson's vote for desegregation, have the potential to create transformational experiences. These are "epiphanies" (see Sams, 1994). In these moments, personal character is manifested and made apparent. By recording these experiences in detail, researchers are able to illuminate the moments of crisis that occur in individuals' lives. Such moments are often interpreted, both by the persons who have them and by others, as turning-point experiences (Strauss, 1959). Having had such a moment, a person is never quite the same again.

Perhaps an example will clarify the concept of epiphany. In the Christian religion, the Epiphany is a festival, observed on January 6, commemorating the manifestation of Christ to the Gentiles in the persons of the Magi. In this sense, the epiphany is a manifestation or sign of the Christian deity. Now consider the following moment in the life of the late Martin Luther King, Jr. On the night of January 27, 1956, King, at the age of 26, had received several telephone threats on his life. Unable to sleep, doubting his place in the Montgomery Bus Boycott and his leadership position in the Southern Christian Leadership Conference, he sat alone at his kitchen table. As he sat there, he heard an inner voice that he identified as Jesus Christ.

King later stated: "I heard the voice of Jesus. . . . He promised never to leave me, never to leave me alone." The historian Howell Raines (1986) comments on David J. Garrow's depiction of this incident in Garrow's biography of King:

> Other biographers have noted this episode, but Mr. Garrow asks us to regard it as the transforming moment, the most important night in his life, the one he always would think back to in future years when the pressures seemed to be too great. (p. 33)

Garrow emphasizes that King returned again and again in his later life to this epiphany, referring to it as "the vision in the kitchen."

In *The Dubliners,* James Joyce employs the method of depicting the epiphany. Indeed, Joyce later described his original notes for the book as epiphanies. Levin (1976) discusses Joyce's use of this technique:

> Joyce underscored the ironic contrast between the manifestation that dazzled the Magi and the apparitions that manifest themselves on the streets of Dublin; he also suggested that these pathetic and sordid glimpses . . . offer a kind of revelation. As the part, significantly chosen, reveals the whole, a word or detail may be enough to exhibit a character or convey a situation. (p. 18)

The following passage from "Counterparts," a story in *The Dubliners,* reveals how Joyce (1914/1976a) used this method:

> A very sullen-faced man . . . was full of smouldering anger and revengefulness. . . . He cursed everything. . . .
>   His wife was a little sharp-faced woman who bullied her husband when he was sober and was bullied by him when he was drunk. . . . A little boy came running down the stairs.
>   —Who is that? said the man. . . .

—Me, pa. . . .
—Where's your mother? . . .
—What's for my dinner? . . .
. . . You let the fire out! By God, I'll teach you to do that again! . . .
He . . . seized the walkingstick. . . .
—I'll teach you to let the fire out! . . .
The little boy cried *O, pa!* And ran whimpering around the table, but the
man . . . caught him by the coat. . . .
—Now, you'll let the fire out the next time! said the man, striking at him
viciously with the stick. Take that, you little whelp! (pp. 108-109)

In this excerpt, Joyce reveals how the father's violence and anger are di-
rected toward his child. In the interaction, the man's violent character is
revealed.

Consider another form of family or domestic violence, wife battering.
Here is an example of an epiphany as it is displayed in the life of a battered
Korean wife. This woman is now separated from her husband.

I have been beaten so many times severely in the early days of the marriage. But I would tell you the recent one. About 8 months ago, I was
beaten badly. In the middle of the beating I ran out of the house. . . . But he
followed and caught me. He grabbed my hair and dragged me to the house.
He pushed me into the bathroom and kicked my body with his foot. My
baby was crying. . . . Now I suffer from a severe headache. When I go out to
the grocery store, I can't see items. I feel pain in my eyes. And I feel
dizzy. . . . I can't forgive him! I hate, hate, hate him so much. . . . Is this
because I was born a woman? (quoted in Cho, 1987, p. 236)

Another battered wife describes her experiences in the following words:

He didn't let me sleep. We sat in the living room together from midnight till
early in the morning. He forced me to sit down on the sofa while he drank
beers. This went on for about a month. Every night he said the same story.
It was like to turn on the recorder. He said that I am a ruthless bitch. He said
he doubted if I was a virgin when I married him. . . . In the early days of the
marriage, he used to force me to be naked and then he drank looking at me.
Then he told me to dance. (quoted in Cho, 1987, p. 231)

In these excerpts victims of family violence vividly report how they experienced battering. Their words bring the experience alive. These experiences became part of the turning-point moments in their relationships with
their husbands. Cho (1987) connects these experiences to the subsequent
dissolution of the women's marriages.

Types of Epiphanies

There are four forms of epiphany: the major, the cumulative, the minor and illuminative, and the relived (see Chapter 8). In the major epiphany, an experience shatters a person's life, making it never the same again. The murder that Raskolnikov commits in *Crime and Punishment* is an example. The cumulative epiphany occurs as the result of a series of events that have built up in the person's life. For example, a women, after years of battering, murders her husband or files for divorce. In the minor or illuminative epiphany, underlying tensions and problems in a situation or relationship are revealed. Cho's (1987) account of the wife who was repeatedly battered by her husband illustrates this form of the epiphany. As the woman stated, she had been beaten many times in the early days of her marriage. In the relived epiphany, the individual relives, or goes through again, a major turning-point moment in his or her life. The Korean women quoted above were reliving their battering experiences with their husbands.

Locating the Epiphany

The epiphany occurs in those problematic interactional situations where the individual confronts and experiences a crisis. Often a personal trouble erupts into a public issue, as when a battered woman flees her home and calls the police, or an alcoholic enters a treatment center for alcoholism.

Epiphanies occur within the larger historical, institutional, and cultural arenas that surround an individual's life. The interpretive scholar seeks, as C. Wright Mills (1959) observes, to understand "the larger historical scene in terms of its meaning for the inner life and the external career of a variety of individuals" (p. 5). Thus the scholar must connect personal problems and personal troubles to larger social, public issues. Troubles are personal matters, such as becoming an alcoholic or being a battered wife. Issues have to do with public matters and institutional structures, such as treatment centers for alcoholism or shelters for battered women. Troubles, Mills states,

occur within the character of the individual and within the range of his immediate relations with others; they have to do with his self and those limited areas of social life of which he is directly and personally aware. . . . A trouble is a private matter: values cherished by an individual are felt by him to be threatened. (p. 8)

Issues, on the other hand,

have to do with matters that transcend these local environments of the individual and the range of his inner life. They have to do with the organization of many such milieux into the institutions of an historical society as a whole. . . . An issue is a public matter: some value cherished by publics is felt to be threatened. (p. 8)

Our task, Mills argues, is to learn how to relate public issues to personal troubles and to the problems of the individual life (p. 226).

Troubles are always biographical. Public issues are always historical and structural. Biography and history thus join in the interpretive process. This process always connects an individual life and its troubles to a public historical social structure. Personal troubles erupt in moments of individual and collective crisis. They are illuminated, often in frightening detail, in the epiphanies of a person's life. These existential crises and turning-point encounters thrust the person into the public arena. His or her problem becomes a public issue.

Strategically, the researcher locates epiphanies in those interactional situations where personal troubles become public issues. The researcher works backward, from the public to the private, seeking out persons whose troubles have come to the public's attention. Cho (1987), for example, located battered women by going to a center for battered women in Seoul, Korea. In my own studies of alcoholism, I worked backward from treatment centers and Alcoholics Anonymous meetings to the personal lives of alcoholics (Denzin, 1987a, 1987b).

Liminality, Ritual, and the Structure of the Epiphany

Epiphanies are experienced as social dramas, as dramatic events with beginnings, middles, and endings. Epiphanies represent ruptures in the structure of daily life. Victor Turner (1986b, p. 41), reminds us that the theater of social life is often structured around a fourfold processual ritual model involving "breach," "crisis," "redress," and "reintegration" or "schism." Each of these phases is organized as a ritual. Redressive rituals, for example, "include divination into the hidden causes of misfortune, conflict, and illness" (p. 41).

Many rituals are associated with life-crisis ceremonies, "particularly those of puberty, marriage, and death." Turner (1986b) contends that redressive and life-crisis rituals "contain within themselves a liminal phase, which provides a stage . . . for unique structures of experience" (p. 41). Liminal phases of experience are detached from daily life and are characterized by the presence of ambiguous and monstrous images, sacred symbols, ordeals, humiliation, gender reversals, tears, struggle, joy, and remorse (p. 41). The liminal phase of experience is a kind of no-person's land "betwixt and between the structural past and the structural future" (p. 41). Epiphanies are ritually structured liminal experiences, connected to moments of breach, crisis, redress, and reintegration or schism.

Universal Singulars

Interpretive interactionism assumes that every human being is a universal singular (Sartre, 1981, p. ix). No person is ever just an individual. He or she must be studied as a single instance of more universal social experiences and social processes. The person, Sartre (1981) states, is "summed up and for this reason universalized by his epoch, he in turn resumes it by reproducing himself in it as a singularity" (p. ix). Every person is like every other person but like no other person. Interpretive studies, with their focus on the epiphany, attempt to uncover this complex interrelationship between the universal and the singular, between private troubles and public issues in a person's life. In this way, all interpretive studies are biographical and historical. They are always fitted to the historical moment that surrounds the subjects' life experiences.

WHAT IS INTERPRETIVE
INTERACTIONISM?

Interpretive research has the following characteristics: (a) It is existential, interactional, and biographical; (b) it is naturalistic; (c) it is based on sophisticated rigor; (d) it can be both pure and applied; (e) it is anchored in the seventh moment and builds on feminist critiques of positivism; and (f) it is concerned with the social construction of gender, power, knowledge, history, and emotion. Discussion of each of these points is required.

The Existential, Interactional Text

The interactional text (Goffman, 1983) is present whenever an individual is located in a social situation. It is ubiquitous. It is interaction itself. Interpretive researchers collect and analyze existentially experienced, interactional texts. This is called doing existential ethnography (see Chapter 8).

The works of Goffman (1959, 1961a, 1961b, 1967, 1971, 1974, 1981) and Garfinkel (1967; Garfinkel, Lynch, & Livingston, 1981) and their students are commonly associated with the study of face-to-face interaction and its interpretation. These researchers have approached this topic from dramaturgical, linguistic, structural, cultural, and phenomenological per-spectives. They have shown how the world in front of us can be read and interpreted in terms of the rituals and taken-for-granted meanings that are embedded in the interaction process. They have disrupted this order so as to expose its underlying normative assumptions. They have stressed its so-cially constructed nature and have examined its fragile features. They have connected the micro world of interaction to the larger, macro structures of society, including gender, race and ethnicity, work, medicine, psychiatry, science, and play and leisure.

There are four problems with this body of work as it bears on the interpre-tive agenda. First, it is nonbiographical and ahistorical. It does not locate interactional texts within the larger, historical social structure. Second, it seldom addresses existentially meaningful or relevant interactional experi-ences (but see Garfinkel, 1967, pp. 116-185; Goffman, 1961b, 1983). Third, it inserts externally derived conceptual schemes into the reading of the inter-action text. Fourth, it typically reads interaction texts in terms of broader structural and ritual issues. It seldom deals with the problems at hand as these problems are addressed by the interactants in question. (Garfinkel has often avoided these last two problems, especially when he has dealt with breaches or disruptions in interaction. These problems are prevalent through-out Goffman's work, however.) Goffman and Garfinkel adopt a structural, impersonal view of interactants and interaction. They study "moments and their persons," not "persons and their moments of interaction."

Idiographic and Nomothetic Research

The approach that Garfinkel and Goffman take to the interaction text is *nomothetic* (Allport, 1942) and *etic* (Pike, 1954) rather than *idiographic* (Allport, 1942) and *emic* (Pike, 1954). Nomothetic studies seek abstract generalizations about phenomena and often offer nonhistorical explana-tions. Etic investigations are external. They are often comparative and cross-cultural; they assume, that is, that the processes being studied tran-scend culture. Etic studies seek the discovery of general patterns. For Goffman this might be facework rituals; for Garfinkel, it might be the opera-tion of the *et cetera* rule in conversations. Specific configurations of mean-ing that operate within a single case or culture are set aside in favor of cross-case universals.

Idiographic research assumes that each individual case is unique. This means that every interactional text is unique and shaped by the individuals who create it. This requires that the voices and actions of individuals must be heard and seen in the texts that are reported. Emic studies are also idiographic. They seek to study experience from within, through the use of thick description, narratives and accounts that attempt to capture the meanings and experiences of interacting individuals in problematic situations. They seek to uncover the conceptual categories persons use when they interact with one another and create meaningful experience. Emic investigations are particularizing. Etic research is generalizing. Interpretive interactionist studies are idiographic and emic. They reject the nomothetic, etic impulse to abstract and generalize. For these reasons there is only limited utility in the etic, nomothetic approaches to the interactional text taken by Goffman and Garfinkel. Although their works establish the structural regularities present in interaction, their ahistorical, nonbiographical stance does not permit the discovery of what a particular interactional moment means to its interactants. Their ability to speak to the epiphany, or to the moment of existential crisis in a person's life, is thereby severely restricted. Although they may be able to reveal the structure of such moments, they are unable to reveal their meanings to the participants in question.

The Progressive-Regressive Method of Sartre

For the above reasons, I advocate the adoption of a different approach to the reading of the interactional text. I have elsewhere recommended the use of Sartre's (1963, pp. 85-166) progressive-regressive method of analysis (see Denzin, 1984a, p. 183). I have also termed this the *critical interpretive method.*

The progressive-regressive method seeks to situate and understand a particular class of subjects within a given historical moment. Progressively, the method looks forward to the conclusion of a set of acts or actions undertaken by a subject, such as Mrs. Anderson's vote, the murder committed by Raskolnikov, or the battering of a Korean wife. The term *progressive* refers here to the forward, temporal dimension of the interpretation process. Regressively, the method works back in time to the historical, cultural, and biographical conditions that moved the subject to take or to experience the actions being studied. By moving forward and backward in time, the researcher situates the subject's projects and actions in time and space. The unique features of the subject's life are illuminated in the interactional episodes that are studied. The similarities and commonalities that the subject shares with others are also revealed.

Literary Naturalism

Interpretive interactionists employ a strategy of research that implements interpretive interactionism in concrete research and policy-making situations (see Ryan, Greene, Lincoln, Mathison, & Mertens, 1998). This method of research is naturalistic and employs the narrative methods of literary journalism (see Richardson, 2000, p. 931). It is located in the natural worlds of everyday social interaction. It tells stories. It relies upon "sophisticated rigor" (Denzin, 1989b, pp. 234-235), which is the researcher's commitment to make his or her interpretive materials and methods as public as possible. Indeed, sophisticated rigor describes the work of any and all researchers who employ multiple methods, seek out diverse empirical situations, and attempt to develop interpretations and personal stories grounded in the worlds of lived experience. It builds out of the case study, biographical, ethnographic approach advocated by Stake (1978, 2000) and others. It goes beyond the single-case method to the analysis of multiple cases, life stories, life histories, and self-stories. It utilizes the full range of biographical-interpretive methods to be discussed in Chapter 3.

Types of Interpretive Researchers

There are two basic types of interpretive researchers. Some, such as Geertz (1973, 1983, 1988), Strauss (1987), and Becker (1986), engage in *pure interpretation* for the purposes of building meaningful interpretations of social and cultural problematics. Ortner (1997a, p. 5) calls this a focus on issues of social moral philosophy. These scholars aim to construct interpretations that are grounded in social interaction. For example, Strauss's work on chronic illness and medical technology has as its goal a grounded theory that "accounts for a pattern of behavior which is relevant and problematic for those involved" (Strauss, 1987, p. 34). Becker's studies of how schools fail to teach students to learn are examples of pure interpretation that becomes evaluation (see Becker, 1986, pp. 173-190).

This kind of work (Strauss's and Becker's) can inform the second type of interpretive work, which is *interpretive evaluation,* or what Ortner (1997a, p. 5) describes as addressing current social problems. Such researchers engage in policy-making research. They conduct research on "a fundamental social problem in order to provide policymakers with pragmatic, action-oriented recommendations for alleviating the problem" (Majchrzak, 1984, p. 12). Interpretive evaluation research is conducted from the point of view of the person experiencing the problem; it sides not with policy makers, but with the underdogs for whom policy makers make policies (Becker, 1973). This does not mean, however, that the point of view of the policy maker cannot be considered. This can be the case in those situations where others are criticizing and forming policy for policy makers. Interpretive interactionists are committed moral thinkers. They explore, from a feminist, communitarian ethical perspective, the complex interrelationship between moral philosophy and current social problems.

What Interpretive Researchers Can Do

As I have argued in Chapter 1, research of this order can produce meaningful descriptions and interpretations of social processes. It can offer explanations of how certain conditions came into existence and why they persist. Interpretive evaluation research can also furnish the basis for realistic proposals concerning the improvement or removal of certain events or problems (see Becker & Horowitz, 1986, p. 85).

Interpretive evaluation researchers who do this kind of work are often partisans for one point of view (radical, conservative), whereas others becomes state counselors (i.e., they work for the government). Silverman (1985, p. 180) has discussed the problems associated with this latter approach; often such sociologists become agents of the state and are unable to conduct their research in a completely free fashion.

Of course, all researchers take sides, or are partisans for one point of view or another. Value-free interpretive research is impossible. This is the case because every researcher brings his or her own preconceptions and interpretations to the problem being studied (Gadamer, 1975; Heidegger, 1927/1962). The term *hermeneutical circle* or *hermeneutical situation* (Heidegger, 1927/ 1962, p. 232) refers to this basic fact of research. All scholars are caught in the circle of interpretation. They can never be free of the hermeneutical situation. This means that researchers must state beforehand their prior interpretations of the phenomena they intend to investigate. Unless they clarify these meanings and values, the effects of the research on subsequent interpretations will remain clouded and may often be misunderstood.

Postpositivism and the Assumptions of Detached Research

Traditional sociological research, in its various forms, has assumed that social processes, experimentally and quasi-experimentally defined, have effects on real-world affairs. These effects are assumed to be objectively measurable through the collection of quantitative data drawn from the world under study. By objectifying the observational process, this model divorces the researcher from the world under study.

This model presumes that social processes can be captured within the strict cause-and-effect paradigm of positivism (Lincoln & Guba, 1985, pp. 24-28) and quasi-experimentalism (Lieberson, 1985). This research paradigm, as I have argued in Chapter 1, assumes the following:

1. "Objective" reality can be captured.
2. The observer can be separated from what is observed.
3. Observations and generalizations are free from situational and temporal constraints; that is, they are universally generalizable.
4. Causality is linear, and there are no causes without effects and no effects without causes.
5. Inquiry is value-free.

(For discussion of each of these points, see Lincoln & Guba, 2000.)

INTERPRETATION AND SCIENCE

Clearly, the interpretive perspective in the seventh moment is post-positivist and critical (Lincoln & Guba, 2000).[2] This perspective opposes each of the above assumptions for the following reasons.

1. Logical positivism and scientific sociology have historically assumed that the language of the natural sciences should and can be the language of the human sciences. This assumption holds that references to the social world that cannot be verified under quantifiable, observable, scientifically controlled conditions must be, following Wittgenstein's (1922) dictum, "passed over in silence" (p. 151). Statements regarding human subjectivity, intentionality, and meaning are superficially treated or excluded from the positivist's domain. Interpretive interactionism is founded on the study, expression, and interpretation of subjective human experience.

2. Positivistic sociology seeks causal explanations of social phenomena. It does so through the use of a variable-analytic language that is largely divorced from everyday life. Interpretive interactionism rejects causal modes and methods of analysis. The search for causal "whys," causal paths, causal chains, and causal antecedents is detrimental to the study and understanding of directly lived experience.

3. The "why" question is replaced by the "how" question. That is, how is social experience, or a sequence of social interaction, organized, perceived, and constructed by interacting individuals? How, then, not why.

4. Positivistic sociology presupposes a theoretical-analytic conceptual framework that stands independent of the world of interacting individuals. This framework, whether derived from classical or contemporary theory (Marx, Durkheim, Simmel, Weber, Freud, Parsons, Merton, Habermas, or Giddens), assumes that human behavior can be meaningfully categorized and analyzed within the conceptual elements of an abstract, grand, or middle-range theory. Lived experience and its meanings drop out of positivistic social science to be replaced by such complex variable terms as *base, super-structure, division of labor, bureaucracy, ego function, functional prerequisite, distorted communication,* and *the latent consequences of purposive action.* These second-order concepts divorce human reality from the scientist's scheme of analysis.

More is going on in this framework, for it presumes the "notion of a single standpoint from which a final overriding version of the world can be written." This standpoint presumes a universal sociological subject, the white male. It presumes a view outside society and argues that society can be written about from the position of an objective observer (Smith, 1989, p. 44). This observer-as-a-social-theorist creates a discourse that suspends the presence of a real subject in the world. It makes social experience irrelevant to the topic at hand. It creates an interpretive structure that says social phenomena should be interpreted as social facts (Smith, 1989, p. 45). It shifts arguments about agency, purpose, meaning, and intention from the subject to the phenomena being studied. It then transforms those phenomena into texts about society, giving the phenomena a presence that rests in the textual description (Smith, 1989, p. 45). Real live people then enter the text as a figment of discourse in the form of excerpts from field notes or the casual observations of the theorist, or as "ideal types" (Smith, 1989, p. 51).

Feminist standpoint theorists wish to overturn this picture of social science. They begin from the perspective of women's experiences, experiences shaped by a gender-based division of labor that has excluded women from the public sphere. A feminist standpoint is thus constructed, building, as Clough (1994, p. 74) argues, on women's identities in the private sphere (housewife, homemaker, mother, daughter), working outward to women's identities in the public sphere (secretary, administrative assistant, Marxist-feminist social scientist, filmmaker, writer). Not only do women know differently than men, women's experiences should be the starting point for a more accurate representation of reality (Clough, 1994, p. 74). This starting point will erase the public/private distinction in everyday life. It will lead to the production of local, gendered knowledge about the workings of the world. It will show how the patriarchal apparatus structures this daily life through the reproduction of text-mediated discourses (D. Smith, 1993).

5. Interpretive interactionism aims, as much as possible, for a concept-free mode of discourse and expression. Its mode of expression is locked into the *first-order, primary, lived concepts of everyday life.* Following Merleau-Ponty (1973), descriptive phenomenology and interpretive interactionism attempt to render understandable the "prose of the world." Such a rendering assumes that the streams of situations and experience that make up everyday life will not submit to experimental, statistical, comparative, or causal control and manipulation. Every human situation is novel, emergent, and filled with multiple, often conflicting, meanings and interpretations. The interpretivist attempts to capture the core of these meanings and contradictions. Interpretive interactionism assumes that the languages of ordinary people can be used to explicate their experiences.

Biography and Inquiry

This world does not stand still, nor will it conform to the scientist's logical schemes of analysis. It contains its own dialectic and its own internal logic. An observer can discover this meaning only through participation in the world. The world does not stand independent of perception or observer organization. In these respects, interpretive interactionists find that their own worlds of experience are proper subject matter for inquiry. Unlike the positivists, who separate themselves from the worlds they study, the interpretivists participate in the social world so as to understand and express its emergent properties and features more fully. Mills (1959) states this position as follows: "The most admirable thinkers within the scholarly community . . . do not split their work from their lives. . . . What this means is that you must learn to use your life experiences in your intellectual work" (pp. 195-196).

Interpretive interactionism asserts that meaningful interpretations of human experience can come only from those persons who have thoroughly immersed themselves in the phenomena they wish to interpret and understand. There is, as Merleau-Ponty (1973) argues, an inherent indeterminateness in the worlds of experience. Systems that attempt to resolve this indeterminateness by going outside the directly experienced realms of everyday life are simply inappropriate for interpretive purposes.

6. The formulation of causal propositions that can be generalized to non-observed populations (based on the extensive analysis of randomly se-

lected samples) is a cardinal feature of much current social science work. Interpretivists reject generalization as a goal and never aim to draw randomly selected samples of human experience. They follow Stake's (1978) position on this issue: "Case studies will often be the preferred method . . . because they are epistemologically in harmony with the reader's experience and thus to that person a natural basis for generalization" (p. 5). Interpretive researchers seek to build interpretations that call forth for readers naturalistic generalization. For the interpretivist, any instance of problematic social interaction, if thickly described (Geertz, 1973; Ortner, 1997b) and connected to a personal trouble, represents a slice of experience that is proper subject matter for interpretive inquiry.

The slices, sequences, and instances of social interaction that the interpretivist studies carry layers of meaning, nuance, substance, and fabric, and these layers come in multiples and are often contradictory. Some flow from other people's histories and some are of an individual's own making. The knowledge and control structures that lie behind these meaning experiences must be uncovered in an interpretive investigation. Every topic of investigation must be seen as carrying its own logic, sense of order, structure, and meaning. Like a novelist or painter, the interpretivist moves the reader back and forth across the text of his or her prose. In so doing, the researcher makes recognizable and visible a slice of human experience that has been captured.

The Feminist Critique of Positivism

The feminist critique of positivism locates gender asymmetry at the center of the social world (Olesen, 2000). It makes the doing of gender a basic focus of research. The gender stratification system in any social situation creates dominance and power relations that typically reduce women to subordinate positions. Scholars must study how this works. There is no gender-free knowledge. The feminist critique suggests that objective knowledge is not possible. It argues that knowledge should be used for emancipatory purposes. Feminist research, like interpretive interactionism, is critical, biographical, and naturalistic. It seeks to build upon recent developments in postmodern, poststructuralist social theory. Feminist research demands that the voices of women speak in and through the interpretive text.

To summarize, a critical understanding and interpretation of everyday life must consider the gendered, situated, structural, and practical features of that world. Requirements for the researcher may be stated thus:

1. Utilize multiple case study, biographical methods.

2. Find the crises and epiphanies in the subjects' lives.

3. Connect these experiences, as personal troubles, to public issues and institutional formations.

4. Employ sophisticated rigor.

5. Present the phenomenon to be evaluated in the language, feelings, emotions, and actions of those being studied.

6. Follow the five steps of interpretation: deconstruction, capture, bracketing, construction, and contextualization (to be discussed later in this chapter and in Chapter 3).

7. Clearly state one's value position on the phenomenon being evaluated.

Interpretive Criteria for Evaluative Studies

When the project is a program evaluation study, the researcher should add the following to the above list:

1. Collect personal experience stories from the persons in charge of the program (volunteers, caregivers, paid professionals) and from the persons served by the program.

2. Identify the different definitions (local and scientific) of the problem and the program under evaluation.

3. Identify the moral biases that structure the definitions of the problem and the program.

4. Identify the competing models of truth (rationality and emotionality) that operate in the setting.

5. Collect thick descriptions/inscriptions of client and caregiver experiences.

6. Present the phenomena to be evaluated in the language, feelings, emotions, and actions of those being studied.

7. Formulate analytic and thick interpretations of the program based on the local theories of each of the categories of persons in the situation.

8. Formulate understandings of the program based on these interpretations.

9. Compare and contrast local and scientific interpretations and understandings of the program.

10. Show how statistical analyses distort and gloss the actual work of the program.

11. Make proposals for change based on the fit between lived experiences (successes, failures) and the possibilities for change that exist within the program being evaluated.

Researchers who follow such guidelines make it possible for other researchers to evaluate their work. These guidelines also serve to organize interpretive evaluation studies, which are value-laden and take the side of the client in any setting.

The process of interpretation is shaped by history, power, emotionality, and beliefs concerning knowledge. It is to these topics that I now turn.

HISTORY, POWER, EMOTION, AND KNOWLEDGE

History

History enters the research process in four ways. First, the events and processes that are studied unfold over time. In this sense they have their own inner sense of history, or temporality. Second, these events occur within a larger historical social structure. This structure shapes, influences, and constrains the processes under investigation. This structure includes language (in its various formations), micro and macro power relationships, and taken-for-granted cultural meanings that structure everyday social interactions and social experiences. Third, history operates at the level of individual history and personal biography. Each individual brings a personal history to the events that are under investigation. Fourth, the researcher has a personal historical relationship to the interpretive process, as noted above. This personal history also shapes research.

The researcher in any interpretive study must take these four forms of history into account. Too often, the artificial constraints of research design ignore the temporal and historical dimensions of the phenomena being interpreted. As a consequence, the research process becomes trivialized and artificial.

Power

History interacts with power and emotionality. Power permeates every structure of society. Power is embedded in the micro gender relations that make up everyday life (Foucault, 1980, 2000). As Foucault (2000, p. 343) has noted, power circulates through the local capillaries and circuits of power relationships in a society. Power is force and domination. It may, in certain circumstances, take the form of violence. Power exists as a process, in the dominance relations between men and women and in the relations between groups and institutions. Power is force or interpersonal dominance actualized in human relationships through manipulation and control. It often involves the destruction of one human being by another. Power both creates and destroys. It creates new social formations while it destroys existing social structures. Recall, for example, the quotations above from Cho's (1987) study of Korean wives battered by their husbands.

Interpretive research inevitably involves power. Discourses on truth and knowledge are implicated in relations of power. Researchers are often given power to enter situations and make interpretations. In turn, they report their interpretations to others who hold power positions, and their interpretations often work their way back into the original situations. New social arrangements are implemented as a result.

Micro power relations permeate every aspect of research. They exist at the level of the researcher who gains access to the field situation in order to make observations. They exist, as a matter of course, in the world that is studied, for it is structured and organized in terms of authority relations. They exist in terms of the research formats, observational methods, and experimental and quasi-experimental research designs the investigator employs. Science enters the research setting as power-in-practice; that is, the researcher carries the power and prestige of science into the field.

Meanings and Effects

As Ortner (1997b) notes, Foucault insists that we look at "cultural forms and practices not in terms of their 'meanings' . . . but in terms of their effects both on those to whom they are addressed and on the world in which they circulate" (p. 137). For example, the practices of Alcoholics Anonymous give persons a language for describing themselves as alcoholics. These practices are connected to steps that lead to the production of certain subject positions. The effects of the discourse are seen in the subjects it produces. This focus on effects helps illuminate the importance of power within any system of discourse. It also helps delineate the places of meaning in such systems. Symbolic orders and systems of meaning are always embedded in systems of domination and power. Understanding the actor's point of view is central to this process.

Emotion

Close inspection reveals that emotionality is everywhere present in interpretive research. It is present in the moods and feelings individuals bring to a study. It is present in the lives of those who are studied. It is present in the interactions that go on between researchers and subjects. It is present in the observations that are gathered. It is part of power and of being powerful, or powerless. An anatomy of power and feeling in the interpretive study reveals that detached, unemotional, purely cognitive interpretation is impossible.

Knowledge

Knowledge is a belief or set of beliefs about a particular segment of reality. Knowledge is socially and politically constructed. Knowledge is intimately related to power. Those who have power create and then define the situations where knowledge is applied. Those with power determine how knowledge about situations is to be gained. Those who have power determine how knowledge will be defined. Those who have power also define what is not knowledge. As Foucault (1980) states: "Knowledge derives not from some subject of knowledge but from the power relations that invest it. . . . All knowledge is political. . . . knowledge has its conditions of possibility in power relations" (p. 220).

Power and Interpretation

Under the positivist paradigm, quantitative, applied, and evaluative knowledge is assumed to be objectively valid. Once obtained, such knowledge is then assumed to have a real force and relevance in the applied social world. Under the interpretive paradigm, knowledge cannot be assumed to be objective or valid in any objective sense. Rather, knowledge reflects interpretive structures, emotionality, and the power relations that permeate the situations being investigated. As a consequence, interpretive studies can reveal only the interpreted worlds of interacting individuals.

THE CRITERIA OF INTERPRETATION

In Chapter 4, I outline in some detail the criteria by which interpretations are evaluated; I review these only briefly here. Extending the discussion in Chapter 1, these criteria include the ability to illuminate the phenomenon, in a thickly contextualized manner, so as to reveal the historical, relational, processual, and interactional features of the experience under study. Interpretation must engulf what is learned about the phenomenon and incorporate prior understandings while always remaining incomplete and unfinished.

These criteria for evaluating interpretations are put in place as the researcher moves through the five phases of the interpretive process: deconstruction, capture, bracketing, construction, and contextualization. *Deconstruction* involves a critical analysis and interpretation of prior studies of the phenomenon in question. *Capture* means that the researcher secures multiple naturalistic instances of the experiences being studied. *Bracketing,* or *reduction,* leads the researcher to attempt to isolate the key or essential features of the processes under examination, such as the stages of being a battered wife. *Construction* describes the attempt to interpret the event or process fully— for example, putting together in a single case all the steps involved in being a battered wife. *Contextualization* occurs when the researcher locates the phenomenon back in the worlds of lived experienced. Cho (1987, 1988), for example, located the instances of battering she had recorded back in the marriages of the Korean women she had studied.

As the researcher enters the interpretive process, he or she is always located within the hermeneutic circle. The researcher, that is, can never get outside of the interpretive process. He or she is always part of what is being studied.

Situating Interpretation

In Chapters 3 and 4, I will examine how an interpretive study is situated in the natural social world. This includes finding and mapping the research site. It also involves connecting social types and biographies to research sites. The researcher must learn the language spoken in the field setting. He or she must also uncover the rituals and routines that structure interaction in the field setting. Interpretation connects biographies to the interactions and performances that occur within social groups.

Thick Description

Thick description attempts to rescue the meanings and experiences that have occurred in the field situation. It captures the interpretations persons bring to the events that have been recorded. It reports these interpretations as they unfold during the interaction. It establishes the grounds for thick interpretation. Thick interpretation attempts to uncover the meanings that inform and structure the subject's experiences. It is the interpretation of thick description. It takes the reader to the heart of the experience that is being interpreted. It assumes that all meaning is symbolic and operates at both the surface and the depths, at both the micro and the macro levels. It turns on thick description, which always joins biography to lived experience. Understanding the individual's perspective is "central to the interpretive practice of 'thick description' " (Ortner, 1997b, p. 158). This model helps us better understand the "cultural construction of 'agency' in particular times and places *and* provides one of the more promising points of departure for theorizing agency as such" (p. 158).

Interpretation and Understanding

Interpretation is the process of setting forth the meaning of an event or experience. Meaning is defined in terms of the intentions and actions of a person. It refers to the intended interpretation (and interpretr) of a symbol (Peirce, 1963, p. 108). Meaning is triadic. It involves interns among (a) a person; (b) an object, event, or process; and (c) the action toward that object, event, or process (see Blumer, 1969, p. 9). Meaning teractional and interpretive. Interpretation clarifies meaning. It may tra e what is said in one language into the meanings and codes of another lage. Interpretation brings out the meaning embedded in a text or in a sl f interaction. Understanding is the process of comprehending and grasp what has been interpreted in a situation or text (see Ricoeur, 1979, p. 96). Telers in a foreign country, for instance, often cannot understand requests that are made of them until they are able to translate those requests into their native language. In this simple example the processes of interpretation and understanding are at work.

Two Types of Description

Description provides the framework for interpretation. That is, an act or process that is to be interpreted must first be described. A description may be thick or thin (Ryle, 1968, pp. 8-9). A thin description simply states facts. For example:

> X drank a cup of coffee at 8:00 a.m., on Tuesday, November 24, 1987, while he wrote a letter to his publisher.

A thick description of the same action might read:

> X, while pouring himself a cup of coffee, remembered that his publisher had requested a letter concerning when his manuscript could be expected. Taking his coffee and cigarettes to his writing table, X began the letter, intending to state in it why he was late with his manuscript and why a new deadline would have to be set. As he wrote the letter, he was interrupted by a phone call from his oldest daughter, who asked him how to insert a word into a computer text. He answered her question and then went back to writing the letter to his publisher. Angry because he felt he had spent too much time on the letter, he dropped his excuses for being late and simply gave the publisher a new date for delivery of his manuscript.

A thick description has the following features: (a) It gives the context of an action, (b) it states the intentions and meanings that organize the action, (c) it traces the evolution and development of the action, and (d) it presents the action as a text that can then be interpreted. A thin description simply

reports fa... dependent of intentions or the circumstances that surround
the action

Types of Interpretation

Interpretation creates the conditions for understanding. There are two
forms of interpretation and understanding: the emotional and the cognitive.
Emotionality and shared experience provide the conditions for deep, authentic understanding. It is this mode of understanding that interpretive
interactionism attempts to build. Cognitive interpretations and understandings lay bare the essential meanings of a phenomenon, but they do not infuse
those meanings with emotion. A mathematical formula, such as Einstein's
special theory of relativity, states the relations between phenomena, but it
does not give emotional meaning to these relations.

Thick description is the cornerstone of interpretation studies. Without it,
authentic understanding would not be possible. This mode of deep understanding emerges as investigators examine negative cases or empirical
irregularities.

THE AGENDA

The heart of interpretive interactionism lies in thick description, thick
interpretation, and deep, authentic understanding. How to write documents
that produce and perform these phenomena is the subject of this book. The
paucity of thick description in the interpretive literature is evident. This
means that students must be taught how to produce thick description and
thick interpretation. At the present time they are not taught such skills; this
situation needs to be corrected.

At the same time, researchers need to undertake projects that utilize interpretive evaluation. Such work will join the study of biography and society in
ways that have been outlined by Mills (1959). It will involve researchers in
drawing upon their own biographical experiences as they formulate their interpretive work. It will require that researchers develop the ability to think
comparatively, historically, and interactionally. It will also dictate that
researchers consider the power and gendered relations that exist in the contexts they study. This concern for power and for how power twists and
shapes human experience gives interpretive research a critical thrust that is
often absent in conventional evaluation studies.

Interpretive researchers should provide thoroughgoing critiques of the
social structures and social processes they investigate. These will include
critiques of the general cultural formations that stand behind the phenom-

ena in question as well as critiques of the intellectual-scientific thought that creates knowledge about the problems examined.

CONCLUSION

In this chapter I have sketched the several sides of interpretive interactionism. Extending Mills (1959), all interpretive studies must, as they draw to conclusion, orient themselves to "the terrible and magnificent world of human society" (p. 225) in the first years of the 21st century. The sociologist's voice can speak to this world. Sociological research can provide more than a mere record of human experience. To paraphrase Faulkner (1967, p. 724), it can become one of the props, the pillars that help women and men endure and prevail. Our texts should display the agonies, the pains, the successes, and the deeply felt human emotions of love, dignity, pride, honor, and respect. This means, of course, that we have no claim over the lives, the experiences, and the stories we tell. We are interlopers. What is told to us is given provisionally, if it is given at all. These lives and experiences remain, always, the lives and stories of those who have told them to us.

One final point: If one's goal is to understand and interpret the world as it is lived, experienced, and given meaning, then one would do well to apply the strategies discussed in this book.

NOTES

1. I conducted this interview along with my colleagues Belden Fields, Walter Feinberg, and Nicole Roberts.

2. An earlier version of the arguments in this section is contained in Denzin (1983, pp. 131-134).

3

Securing
Biographical Experience

This chapter takes up, in turn, the following topics: (a) exemplars of problematic biographical experience; (b) the biographical method and its relation to interpretive interactionism; and (c) the evaluation, reading, and interpretation of biographical materials.

EXEMPLARS

Consider the following story, which was told to the folklorist Sandra Dolby-Stahl, her sister, and her sister-in-law by Sandra's mother, Loretta K. Dolby, as the four women were preparing food for a family picnic. The mother had been a fourth-grade teacher at a small rural school for nearly 20 years.

It's just one of those dumb little things that you tell that doesn't amount to a hill of beans. Only, it was the last day of school and everybody was half crazy anyhow, trying to get everything done. And we had our principal and the P.E. instructor, the coach, there; they were goofing off. And I was sitting there trying my darnedest to get everything caught up. And, everything wasn't going so well. And anyhow, I guess everyone was just sort of knowing what they were doing. These men met in the office there, and every once in a while I could hear them laughing. I knew they were telling dirty jokes and everything. And anyhow, we gals—they'd always shut up when we'd get anywhere close. So right at the end there, here the coach came down there, and he had two great big basketballs. And he rolled them clear down there, and they banged up against my door. And I came out of there and said, "What do you mean rolling your balls down the hall!?" [laughter]
    Those guys—one went that way and one went the other. And pretty soon I heard them burst out laughing, and I went behind my door and slammed the door shut. And I didn't dare show my head out until they'd gone home. . . . Oh, I was embarrassed to death. Crimminee, when he banged those against the door, I came out and said the first thing that came to my

mind. I didn't think it was funny til I realized how it sounded. But they
vanished. (quoted in Dolby-Stahl, 1985, pp. 55-56)

Now consider the following statement. The speaker is a 53-year-old
printer who is attending his second A.A. meeting in 2 years:

I can't get off the dammed stuff by myself. When Dad died he made me
promise that I'd quit. I promised him, but I can't seem to get to where I was
when Dad died. The old man drank a quart of Old Fitzgerald every day for
30 years, then he quit cold when the doctor told him to. My sister's an alcoholic, she can't quit either. The boss says Frank you've got to quit. I try, but
you know I get those shakes in the morning on the way to work. I stop and
get a half-pint of Peppermint Schnapps, so they can't smell it on my breath,
and I drink it and then I quiet down, start to smile, and feel good. It starts to
wear off about the middle of the morning. That's why I keep the cold beer
in the ice chest in the trunk of the car. I go out for a smoke and sneak a beer.
That gets me through to noon. Then I take lunch at Buddie's and have a
couple shots of Schnapps, with the beer that everybody else has. I can
make it through the afternoon. Then I stop after work and really hit it. I get
so shook up about not being able to stop that I seem to drink more. I keep
drinking till I pass out every night. The wife understands, and when I mark
the days off the calendar when I ain't had a drink she's so proud of me. I just
think I ought to be able to do this thing by myself. The old man did. But I
can't. I guess I'll just have to keep coming back to you people. My body's
starting to show the effects now. The Doc says the liver can't take too much
more of this. I don't know, when I take that drink these problems all go
away. But they're there when the drink wears off. Can you people help me?
(quoted in Denzin, 1987a, p. 25)

Next this:

It is by sheer force of work that I am able to silence my innate melancholy.
But the old nature often reappears, the old nature that no one knows, the
deep, always hidden wound. (Gustave Flaubert, October 6, 1864, quoted in
Sartre, 1981, p. x)

The wound to which Flaubert refers is described in a letter written about
Flaubert by a family friend:

My grandmother had taught her elder son to read. She wanted to do as
much for the second and set to work. Little Charlotte at Gustave's
[Flaubert] side learned rapidly; he could not keep up, and after straining to

understand these signs that meant nothing to him, he began to sob. (quoted in Sartre, 1981, p. 3)

Finally, the following:

26 *April:* Mother is putting my new secondhand clothes in order. She prays now, she says, that I may learn in my own life and away from home and friends what the heart is and what it feels. Amen. So be it. Welcome, O life! I go to encounter for the millionth time the reality of experience and to forge in the smithy of my soul the uncreated conscience of my race. (Joyce, 1976b/1916, p. 526)

OVERVIEW

The subject matter of interpretive research is biographical experience. It is carved out of the lives of ordinary men and women. Interpretive studies, as I have argued in Chapter 2, are organized in terms of biographically meaningful events or moments in subjects' lives. Such events—how subjects experience and define them, and how they are woven through the multiple strands of subjects' lives—constitute the focus of interpretive research. Each of the above exemplars speaks to a biographically consequential moment in a person's life. In the first account, Dolby-Stahl's mother recounts a sexually embarrassing experience she had while she was a schoolteacher. In the second story, a printer goes to an A.A. meeting to ask for help with his alcoholism. In the third, Sartre describes a series of pivotal moments in Flaubert's life, involving his slow entry into language. In the fourth, an excerpt from James Joyce's *A Portrait of the Artist as a Young Man,* Joyce conveys Stephen Dedalus's final thoughts as he turns his back on being a priest and departs Ireland for the Continent, to become a writer.

In this chapter I will return to these exemplars as I discuss the biographical method and its relationship to interpretive interactionism. I will distinguish the several forms of the biographical method and then offer a detailed discussion of how interpretations are evaluated in interpretive studies.

NARRATIVE'S MOMENT

We live in narrative's moment (Maines, 1993). The linguistic and textual basis of knowledge about society is now privileged. Everything we study is contained within a storied or narrative representation. The self is a narrative production. There is no separation between self and society. Material social conditions, discourses, and narrative practices interweave to shape the self and its many identities. Narrative's double duty is complex, and self and society are storied productions. This is why narrative is a prime concern of social science today.

Narrative is a telling, a performance event, the process of making or telling a story. A story is an account that involves the narration of a series of events in a plotted sequence that unfolds in time. (*Story* and *narrative* are nearly equivalent terms.) A story has a beginning, a middle, and an ending. Stories have certain basic structural features, including narrators, plots, settings, characters, crises, and resolutions. Experience, if it is to be remembered and represented, must be contained in stories that are narrated. We have no direct access to experience as such. We can study experience only through its representations, through the ways stories are told.

The biographical, interpretive method rests on the collection, analysis, and performance of stories, accounts, and narratives that speak to turning-point moments in people's lives. Narratives are temporal productions (Culler, 1981, p. 187; Ricoeur, 1985, p. 101). The content of a narrative exists independent of its telling, although many narratives can be told only by the persons who experienced the events reported upon. For example, Sandra Dolby-Stahl could not have told the story her mother told, although once having heard her mother's story she can tell it to anyone who will listen. Significant biographical experiences are told and retold in narrative form.

What we take narratives (and stories) to be determines how we will collect and study them. If we define stories as a form of narrative, then we can obtain stories through structured, semistructured, and unstructured interviews, through free association methods, and through collectively produced autobiographies. Methodologically, we can subject narratives-as-stories to content, discourse, cultural, literary, psychoanalytic, formal, structural, semiotic, and feminist analyses. Of course, we can also examine preexisting narratives (myths). On the other hand, stories can be connected to larger narrative structures.

Jean-Paul Sartre (1963) and Holstein and Gubrium (2000, p. 103) remind us that as social constructions, stories always have a larger cultural and historical locus. Individuals are universal singulars, universalizing in their singularity the unique features of their historical moment. Narratives of the self, as temporal constructions, are anchored in local institutional cultures and their interpretive practices. These practices shape how self-narratives are fashioned. Storytellers have agency and self-reflexivity. Their stories are temporal constructions that create the realities they describe. Stories and lives connect and define one another.

However, narratives come in many different forms: contradictory, fragmented, grand, local, institutional. Critical life events are given meaning within various narrative schemes, and they become sites where agency is played out. Indeed, subjects inhabit narrative, even as the self, in its private, public, and gendered versions, is constituted in narrative. And in their narratives, individuals push against prevailing systems of discourse, including those connected to sexuality, family, work, labor, race, intimacy, politics, aging, unemployment, and death. Of course, narratives do not establish the truth of events, nor do they reflect the truth of experience. Narratives create the very events they reflect upon. In this sense, narratives are reflections *on*, not *of*, the world as it is known.

William Kittredge (1996) reminds us that our lives are "ceaselessly intertwined with narrative, with the stories we tell or hear told, those that we dream or imagine or would like to tell. . . . We live immersed in narrative" (p. 157). The stories we tell help us wrestle with the chaos in the world around us, help us to make sense of our lives when things go wrong.

SELVES, NARRATIVES,
AND SACRED PLACES

We live in stories, and we do things because of the characters we become in our tales of self. The narrated self, which is who I am, is a map; it gives me something to hang on to, a way to get from point A to point B in my daily life. But we need larger narratives, stories that connect us to others, to community, to morality and the moral self. At the dawn of a new century, we need new stories.

In his writings on Montana and the West, Kittredge (1996) says that we need new narratives based on new and different ways of performing Montana. He asks for narratives that embed the self in storied histories of sacred spaces and local places. We need to invent new stories for ourselves "in which we live in a society that understands killing the natural world as a way of killing each other. . . . We need a story in which the processes of communality and mutual respect are fundamental" (p. 142). We need stories that encourage us to "understand that the living world cannot be replicated. . . . We need stories that will drive us to care for one another and the world. We need stories that will drive us to action" (pp. 164-165).

Types of Narrative

There are many different forms of narratives: stories in newspapers and magazines, fiction short stories and novels, stories people tell one another about themselves in their everyday lives, stories people tell about other people. Interpretive researchers collect two basic types of narratives: personal experience stories and self-stories. A *personal experience story* is a narrative that relates the self of the teller to a significant set of personal experiences that have already occurred (see Dolby-Stahl, 1985). The story Dolby-Stahl's mother told about the "balls" is a personal experience narrative. The account of Flaubert's learning language is a second-person personal experience story—that is, it is told by another person about Flaubert. A *self-story* is a narrative that creates and interprets a structure of experience as it is being told. The printer's story told at the A.A. meeting is a self-story. He explains events and himself as he tells his story. Joyce's final words in *A Portrait of the Artist* are of the same category; his narrator explains and interprets events as they happen. Self-stories deal simultaneously with the past, the present, and the future, whereas personal experience stories deal only with the past. Self-stories involve ongoing problematic occurrences in their tellers' lives.

A *personal history* is a reconstruction of a life based on interviews, conversations, self-stories, and personal experience stories (see Titon, 1980). Such a history may be focused on the life or biography of a single person, group, or institution. A personal history envelops and embeds self-stories and personal experience stories within a larger narrative structure—the story of a life. One can often glean the full meaning of a personal experience or self-story only by locating the story in the biography of the speaker.

A *testimonio* is a first-person political text told by a narrator who is the protagonist or a witness to the events that are reported upon. *Testimonios* report on torture, imprisonment, social upheaval, colonization processes, and other struggles for survival. These works are intended to produce and record social change. Their truth is contained in the telling of the events that are recorded by the narrators (Beverley, 2000).

Richardson (2000) observes that the narrative genres connected to ethnographic writing have "been blurred, enlarged, altered to include poetry, drama, conversations, readers' theater, and so on" (p. 929). She uses the phrase "creative analytic practice" (CAP) to describe these many different narrative forms, which include autoethnography, fiction stories, poetry, performance texts, polyvocal texts, readers' theater, responsive readings, aphorisms, comedy and satire, visual presentations, allegory, conversation, layered accounts, writing-stories, and mixed genres. Creative nonfiction, performance writing, memoirs, personal histories, and cultural criticism can be added to this list of narrative forms that may be used by the interpretive interactionist.

Process

I will use the term *interpretive biographical method* here to encompass these variations on narratives and stories. The emphasis on self, biography, history, and experience must always work back and forth between a concern for process and the analysis of the specific lives of individuals who live the process that is being studied. The life of the storyteller must always be foremost in the account or interpretation that is written. Process and structure must be blended with lived experiences.

Following Paul Thompson (1978), interpretive biographical materials may be presented in three different ways. First, a researcher may present individual personal experience narratives and connect them to the life story of a given person. Second, a researcher may collect a number of self-stories and personal experience stories grouped around a common theme. Third, a researcher may offer a cross-case analysis of the materials he or she has collected, paying more attention to the process being studied than to the persons whose lives are embedded in those processes.

I would recommend that all interpretive biographical studies incorporate all of the above modes of presentation. Two implications follow. First, the researcher should collect in-depth personal histories. Because any one person can tell multiple stories about his or her life, researchers must understand that individual lives consist of multiple narratives. No self-story or personal experience story will encompass all the stories that could be told about a single life, nor will any personal history contain all the self-stories that could be told about that life. Second, the researcher must secure multiple narratives drawn from the self-stories of many individuals located at different points in the process being interpreted. Such triangulation, or combination of biographical methods, ensures that history, structure, and the individuals studied receive fair and thorough consideration in any inquiry.

The Structuring of Lives

A life encompasses the biographical experiences of a named person. A person is a cultural creation. Every culture, for example, has names for different types of persons: male, female, husband, wife, daughter, son, professor, student, and so on. These names are attached to persons. Persons build biographies around the experiences associated with these names—old man, young man, divorced woman, only daughter, only son, and so on.

These experiences have effects at two levels in a person's life. On the *surface level,* effects are barely felt. They are taken for granted and nonproblematic, as when a person buys a newspaper at the corner grocery store. At the *deep level,* effects cut to the core of the person's life and leave indelible marks. These are the epiphanies of a life. Interpretive researchers attempt to secure self-stories and personal experience stories that deal with events that have had deep-level effects in persons' lives.

All of the stories quoted at the beginning of this chapter speak to events that had lasting effects on individuals' lives. Several years after the events she describes occurred, Dolby-Stahl's mother remembers the day she was embarrassed at her country school by an encounter with the gym teacher, and she shares this sexually embarrassing experience with her daughters and daughter-in-law. The printer tells about key events in his life that he is still dealing with. After *A Portrait of the Artist,* Joyce would write two more books in his attempt to make sense out of his relationships to literature and to Ireland. Flaubert spent a lifetime struggling with his relationship to writing and language.

The Method of Instances

In determining what to observe, an interpretive researcher's initial (and primary) focus should be on the use of the "method of instances" (Psathas, 1995, p. 50). This method takes each instance of a phenomenon as an occurrence that evidences the operation of a set of cultural understandings currently available for use by cultural members.

An analogy may help. Fiske (1994) notes, "In discourse analysis, no utterance is representative of other utterances, though of course it shares structural features with them; a discourse analyst studies utterances in order to understand how the potential of the linguistic system can be activated when it intersects at its moments of use with a social system" (p. 195). This is the argument for the method of instances. The analyst examines those moments when utterances intersect with other utterances, giving rise to an instance of the system in action.

Psathas (1995) clarifies the meaning of *instance:* "An instance of something is an occurrence . . . an event whose features and structures can be examined to discover how it is organized" (p. 50). An occurrence is evidence that "the machinery for its production is culturally available . . . [for example] the machinery of turn-taking in conversation" (pp. 50-51). The analyst's task is to understand how this instance and its intersections work, to show what rules of interpretation are operating, to map and illuminate the structure of the interpretive event itself.

Whether the particular utterance or event occurs again is irrelevant. The question of sampling from a population is also not an issue, for it is never possible to say in advance what an instance or event is a sample of (Psathas, 1995, p. 50). Indeed, collections of instances "cannot be assembled in advance of an analysis of at least one, because it cannot be known in advance what features delineate each case as a 'next one like the last' " (Psathas, 1995, p. 50). This means there is little concern for empirical generalization.

Psathas is clear on this point. The goal is not an abstract or empirical generalization; rather, the concern is "with providing analyses that meet the criteria of unique adequacy" (p. 50). Each analysis must be fitted to the case at hand; each "must be studied to provide an analysis *uniquely adequate* for that particular phenomenon" (p. 51).

Contextualizing Narratives: Interactional Slices

In addition to collecting and writing narratives, interpretive researchers record live interactional sequences. These sequences, if strategically selected, are occasions for the telling of personal experience stories. Researchers can then turn these stories into performance texts.

A 12-Step Call

The following interactional sequence was collected on January 23, 1983. It was reported to me by one of the participants in the situation. The event took place from 10:15 a.m. to 11:30 a.m. The settings are a motel room, an automobile, and a detoxification unit in a substance abuse center. The participants are three men: M., 34 years old, an alcoholic who has relapsed (gone on a drunk) and has called the A.A. hot line for help; P., 43 years old, a recovering alcoholic; and W., 50 years old, another recovering alcoholic who received M.'s telephone call. During the conversation that follows, the interactants are sitting around a table in the detox unit. They have known one another for approximately 8 months. P. and W. are doing what in A.A. is known as a 12-Step call. This means they are helping an alcoholic who has asked for help to stop drinking. Each has nearly a year of sobriety. This conversation, which was recorded, begins as the three men arrive at the detoxification center:

M.: Is that all there is? Is this what being in A.A. is all about?

P.: What do you mean?

M.: [Reaches for a cigarette; hand shakes as he tries to light it.] I don't know. I mean, is this all there is? Go to your damned meetings, read your Big Book, not drink. Stay at home and take care of my mother. Is this all there is?

W.: No, there's more to it than that, but it has to start with not drinking. You can do anything you want to do. Anything. Just don't drink. Hell, my whole life has turned around.

M.: You can take your Big Book and throw it out the window. It don't mean nothin' to me. I mean, *Is this all there is?* My life's like that Peggy Lee song. It ain't got no meanin'. At least when I'm drunk I can be somebody else. I can get out of the old lady's house and be somethin'.

W.: Will the Big Book help me stay sober? They got storie.
and just like yours. Have you read it? Look at you now.)st like mine
all there is? unk. Is this

M.: Man, I can't take it. You know. I just can't take it. I think of
San Diego. I see my mom waiting for me to come home druid wife in
in the bar having fun. I take a drink and I see A.A. faces in the myself
just want to die. Man, I

P.: It doesn't have to be this way, M. It doesn't have to be this wa)
same way you do every time I drank. Give A.A. a chance. It the

The conversation ends at this point. As P. and W. leave the detox unit, is
sitting at the table, holding his head in his hands and crying. He has knock
over his cup of coffee.

The next day, one of the A.A. members who answered M.'s 12-Step call
relates the following story:

> Yesterday I went on a 12-Step call. To a motel. I stayed at the same motel
> once when I went on a week's drunk. It was good for me to go back to that
> place. To see what it's like if you pick up that first drink. I was busy when
> the call came and I didn't want to go. But I'm glad I did. We got into the Big
> Book, into alcoholism, and into my disease. I'm just glad I don't have to
> drink today. This was my first 12-Step call and I was scared as hell. There
> was a bottle of 4 Roses on the table and beer in the sink. Three months ago I
> would have had a drink. I'm sure. I don't think I'll ever forget how I felt in
> that room with that alcoholic who wanted our help. Empty beer cans, the
> smell of whiskey and stale cigarettes, cartoons on the TV. I'm grateful to
> be sober today.

Here an interactional experience becomes the occasion for a personal experience story. Interpretive research attempts to merge the study of ongoing
interaction with the stories that come from such experiences. This is termed
contextualizing a narrative.

Participating, Interviewing, and Listening

Interpretive interactionists attempt to live their way into the lives of those
they investigate. Such researchers attempt to see the world and its problems
as they are seen by the people who live inside particular lives. As a strategy,
this method throws the researcher directly into the social world under investigation. It requires that the researcher make careful records, in field notes,
of the problematic and routine features of that world. An interpretive researcher seeks to discover recurring structural, interactional, and meaning
patterns. The researcher attempts to share in the subjects' world, to partici-

the rounds of activities that make up that world, and to see
pate di the subjects do. The participant observer's goals revolve
that Wtempt to render that world meaningful from the perspective of
aroun d.

those lucting open-ended interviewing, the interpretive researcher
work from a general list of the kinds of information he or she wants
nee from a set of questions to which he or she wishes answers. The re-
to er must alter the phrasing of the questions and the order in which they
sked to fit each individual interviewed. The use of open-ended inter-
ving is based on the assumption that meanings, understandings, and in-
pretations cannot be standardized; they cannot be obtained through the
e of a formal, fixed-choice questionnaire. The interviewer must be a
skilled asker of questions as well as a skilled listener. The strategy of open-
ended interviewing fits naturally with participant observation, interactional
study, and the collection of narratives. It is important to remember that a
good interviewer is simply putting into practice what every good conversa-
tionalist knows how to do. That is, an interview should be a conversation, a
give-and-take between two persons. Douglas (1985) has given the name
"creative interviewing" to this process in which two or more persons cre-
atively and openly share experiences with one another in a mutual search for
greater self-understanding.

A good listener doesn't talk; rather, he or she lets others talk. Interpretive
research requires that the observer become a good listener, a skill that involves several elements. First, a good listener does not gossip. Second, a
good listener does not interrupt. Third, a good listener shares his or her own
experiences, thereby transforming the traditional interviewer-respondent
situation into a conversational interaction. When an interviewer only listens, without sharing, this can create distrust in interviewees. Fourth, a good
listener learns what to listen for. Because the interpretive researcher is seeking personal experience stories and self-stories, he or she should learn how
to be present in social groups and social situations where such stories are
most likely to be told. Fifth, a good listener has to have a reason for being a
listener. This means that he or she has to create an identity in the social
groups he or she is studying.

Faulkner (1940/1964) describes V. K. Ratliff, the narrator of his Snopes
family trilogy (*The Hamlet,* 1940; *The Town,* 1957; and *The Mansion,*
1959), as the person "who knew everything about folks in this country"
(p. 36) but who "didn't even tell himself what he is up to. . . . Not even if he
was lying in bed with himself in the dark of the moon" (p. 321). Ratliff is a
traveling sewing machine salesman who calls on every family in the county.
He knows every family's life story. He knows the problems of every family.

He knows who is in trouble and who is not. He never tells one family what he knows about another. He is a trusted listener. He is a model for the interpretive researcher.

INTERPRETING THE BIOGRAPHICAL

Biographical materials must be interpreted. I recommend the following strategies for such interpretation. First, the researcher should locate the subject or case within the social group being studied (e.g., a recovering alcoholic, a mother telling a story, a writer trying to write). Second, the researcher should identify the problematic act or event that structures the subject's life and capture that act or event within a personal experience story or self-story. Third, the researcher should interpret the basic features of the narrative. Fourth, the researcher should relate those interpretations back to the life in question.

Reading the Narrative and Informed Readers

The interpreter of personal experience stories and self-stories must be an "informed reader" (Dolby-Stahl, 1985, p. 53; Fish, 1980, pp. 48-49). An informed reader (and performer) has the following characteristics: He or she (a) knows the language that is used in the story (e.g., what a 12-Step call is); (b) knows the biography of the storyteller, if only in a partial way; (c) is able to take the teller's perspective in the story; (d) has, ideally, had experiences like those contained in the story; (e) is willing to take full responsibility for his or her interpretation; (f) is conversant with the full range of interpretive theories that could be brought to bear upon the story in question (e.g., psychoanalytic, semiotic, poststructuralist, Marxist, feminist, interactionist, phenomenological); (g) assumes that "the creation of 'meaning' is the reader's response to the document he reads" (Dolby-Stahl, 1985, p. 52); (h) believes that there is no one "true" or "real" meaning of a story; and (i) believes, nonetheless, that each teller of a story is the author of the story, and that his or her meanings must be secured if at all possible.

Steps to Interpretation

Elsewhere, I have suggested that the temporal work of interpretation, or hermeneutics, involves the following steps (Denzin, 1984a, pp. 259-260):

1. Securing the interactional text
2. Displaying the text as a unit

3. Subdividing the text into key experiential units
4. Analyzing each unit linguistically and interpretively
5. Serially unfolding and interpreting the meanings of the text to the participants
6. Developing working interpretations of the text
7. Checking these hypotheses against the subsequent portions of the text
8. Grasping the text as a totality
9. Displaying the multiple interpretations that occur within the text

Dolby-Stahl (1985) follows these steps. She first offers the full narrative of the story and then subdivides the text into key units (the rolling of the balls and so on). She next performs an analysis of key phrases and then connects the meanings of these phrases to other phrases within the story. She develops working interpretations of the text and checks these interpretations against other portions of the text. She treats the story as a totality and places her interpretations against others that could be given to it. This is how a biographical narrative is interpreted.

Dolby-Stahl connects her interpretation to her mother's biography. She uses this biographical knowledge to make sense of the story (her mother's age, her membership in the Church of the Brethren, her position as a country schoolteacher in Indiana). By connecting a story to a biography, the researcher is able to show how interactional experiences make sense only when they are fitted to the lives of their participants. If a researcher ignores biography, he or she will write empty, decontextualized interpretations. Dolby-Stahl, for example, could have read the incident in her mother's story as an instance of obscene folk humor in which "balls" would have been read as a slang term for testicles. She could have then coded this centuries-old usage of the pun by her mother into a standard folklore category and given a "Freudian" reading of the dirty pun (Dolby-Stahl, 1985, p. 56). By linking her interpretation to her mother's personal history, Dolby-Stahl offers an informed reading that is thick and biographically relevant.

Informed readers attempt to treat each storyteller as a universal singular. This is what Dolby-Stahl did with her mother, what Sartre did with Flaubert, and what Joyce did with Stephen Dedalus.

CONCLUSION

In this chapter I have discussed how interpretive researchers study biographical experience. Interpretive researchers collect personal experience stories and self-stories that focus on key, turning-point moments in people's lives and then fit these stories to the personal histories of the storytellers.

Interpretive researchers also collect and analyze interactional slices, which they turn into narratives and sometimes perform, as I have illustrated with my account of Mrs. Anderson's interview in Chapter 2. In Chapter 4, I discuss in greater detail the criteria that should be used in the evaluation of researchers' interpretations.

4

The Interpretive Process

This chapter takes up the following topics: (a) the steps involved in interpretation and (b) criteria for evaluating interpretative materials.

THE STEPS TO INTERPRETATION

There are six phases or steps in the interpretive process. These may be stated as follows:

1. Framing the research question
2. Deconstructing and analyzing critically prior conceptions of the phenomenon
3. Capturing the phenomenon, including locating and situating it in the natural world and obtaining multiple instances of it
4. Bracketing the phenomenon, or reducing it to its essential elements and cutting it loose from the natural world so that its essential structures and features may be uncovered
5. Constructing the phenomenon, or putting the phenomenon back together in terms of its essential parts, pieces, and structures
6. Contextualizing the phenomenon, or relocating the phenomenon back in the natural social world

Discussion of each of these steps is necessary.

Framing the Research Question

The research question is framed by two sources: the researcher and the subject. As I have indicated in Chapter 1, the researcher with a sociological imagination uses his or her own life experiences as topics of inquiry.

The Sociological Imagination

A person with a sociological imagination thinks critically, historically, and biographically. He or she attempts to identify the varieties of men and women who prevail in given historical periods. Such scholars attempt to examine "the major issues for publics and the key troubles for private individuals in our time" (Mills, 1959, p. 11). Persons with a sociological imagination self-consciously make their own experience part of their research. The sociological imagination is not confined only to sociologists. There are also the "political imagination," the "psychological imagination," the "anthropological imagination," the "historical imagination," and the "journalistic or literary imagination" (see Mills, 1959, p. 19). What matters is the researcher's ability to think reflectively, historically, comparatively, and biographically.

Such a researcher is led to seek out subjects who have experienced the types of experiences the researcher seeks to understand. The subject in the interpretive study elaborates and further defines the problem that organizes the research. Life experiences give greater substance and depth to the problem the researcher wishes to study. Given this interpretation of subjects and their relationship to the research question, the researcher's task of conceptualizing the phenomenon to be studied is easily defined. It is contained within the self-stories and personal experience stories of the subjects. The researcher seeks to uncover how the problematic act or event in question organizes and gives meaning to the persons studied.

The question that the researcher frames must be a *how* and not a *why* question. As I have argued in Chapter 2, interpretive studies examine how problematic, turning-point experiences are organized, perceived, constructed, and given meaning by interacting individuals.

The researcher's framing of the research question involves the following steps:

1. Locating, within his or her own personal history, the problematic biographical experience to be studied
2. Discovering how this problem, as a private trouble, is or is becoming a public issue that affects multiple lives, institutions, and social groups
3. Locating the institutional formations or sites where persons with these troubles do things together (Becker, 1986)
4. Beginning to ask not why but how it is that these experiences occur
5. Attempting to formulate the research question into a single statement

*Exemplars: Emotional Experience, the
Alcoholic Self, the Cinematic Racial Order*

In *On Understanding Emotion* (Denzin, 1984a), I focused on a single how question: "How is emotion, as a form of consciousness, lived, experienced, articulated, and felt?" This led to an examination of classical and contemporary theories of emotion, an extended analysis of the essence of emotional experience, and two case studies dealing with family violence and emotionally divided selves. I attempted to answer my *how* question by going to concrete situations where persons interactionally displayed violent emotions.

In *The Alcoholic Self* (Denzin, 1987a) and *The Recovering Alcoholic* (Denzin, 1987b), I asked two how questions: "How do ordinary men and women live and experience the alcoholic self active alcoholism produces?" (1987a, p. 15) and "How is the recovering self of the alcoholic lived into existence?" (1987b, p. 11). These two questions led me to Alcoholics Anonymous, to alcoholic families, and to treatment centers for alcoholism, where I found persons interactionally grappling with the problematics contained in my two how questions.

In my recently completed study of Hollywood's "hood" movies of the 1990s (e.g., *Boyz N the Hood, Menace II Society*), I examined how a cinematic racial order that emphasizes violence, drugs, gangs, and the police is constructed in these films (Denzin, 2001). I compared and contrasted films made by Anglo, Hispanic, and African American filmmakers. This analysis required a historical treatment of the racial order and the factors shaping that order in Hollywood film. I moved back and forth in my analysis from silent film (*The Birth of a Nation*) to the present.

Implementing the How Question

Researchers can implement their how questions in several ways. First, they may bring persons to a research site. Second, they may go to those places where persons with the experience of interest naturally interact. Third, they may study their own interactional experiences. Fourth, they may examine the scientific, biographical, autobiographical, and fictional accounts persons have given of their own or others' experiences with the phenomenon in question (Strauss, 1987). It is advisable for researchers to use as many of these strategies as possible when they begin to implement their how questions.

Deconstructing Prior Conceptions of the Phenomenon

A deconstructive reading of a phenomenon includes a critical analysis of how the phenomenon has been studied and how it is presented and analyzed in the existing research and theoretical literature (see Denzin, 1984a, p. 11; Derrida, 1981, pp. 35-36; Heidegger, 1982, p. 23). Deconstructing a phenomenon involves the following steps:

1. Laying bare prior conceptions of the phenomenon, including how it has been defined, observed, and analyzed
2. Critically interpreting previous definitions, observations, and analyses of the phenomenon
3. Critically examining the underlying theoretical model of human action implied and used in prior studies of the phenomenon
4. Presenting the preconceptions and biases that surround existing understandings of the phenomenon

Exemplar: Battered Wives

Cho's (1987) social phenomenological analysis of Korean family violence provides an example of how deconstruction works. At the time Cho conducted her study, the major theory operating among researchers examining domestic violence was based on social exchange theory. This theory argues that violence is a normal part of family life and that husbands and wives seek to maximize rewards and minimize costs in their exchange relations. It argues that when the husband perceives an imbalance of exchange he becomes violent and uses physical force as a resource to restore equity in the relationship. This theory has been operationalized with a "severity of violence" scale that measures eight forms of violence: throwing things, pushing and shoving, slapping, kicking and hitting, hitting with something, beating up, threatening with a knife or gun, and using a knife or gun.

Social exchange theory predicts that wives will stay in violent relationships when the rewards are greater than the punishments, and they will leave when the punishments are greater than the rewards. Cho (1987) argues that this framework has the following flaws: (a) It is tautologous—there are no independent measures of rewards and costs, other than leaving and staying; (b) it contains no objective measure of the ratio of rewards and punishments; and (c) it contains no way of measuring a wife's subjective definition of the situation. Hence the theory has no predictive or explanatory power.

Methodologically, this theory rests on the assumptions of positivism that I have critiqued in Chapter 2. It assumes that family violence has an objective existence in family life that can be measured on a scale. It assumes that observations can be made free of temporal and situational factors. It presumes a linear model of causality. The theory does not address subjective experience or the interpretive process that structures violent interaction (Denzin, 1984b). It views the wife as a passive agent in the violent marriage.

Cho's deconstructive reading of this literature followed the steps outlined above. She developed an interpretive interactionist view of family violence that built from the accounts battered wives gave of their experiences.

The Hermeneutic Circle

"Inquiry itself is the behavior of the questioner" (Heidegger, 1927/1962, p. 24). The basic concepts and questions the investigator brings to a study are part of the research. They "determine the way in which we get an understanding beforehand of the subject-matter. . . . every inquiry is guided beforehand by what is sought" (Heidegger, 1927/1962, p. 24). An interpretive circle surrounds the research process. Heidegger (1927/1962) argues:

> This circle of understanding is not an orbit in which any random kind of knowledge may move. . . . it is not to be reduced to the level of a vicious circle or even of a circle which is merely tolerated. . . . What is decisive is not to get out of the circle but to come into it the right way. (p. 195)

Interpretive research enters the hermeneutic circle by placing the researcher and the subject in the center of the research process. A double hermeneutic or interpretive circle is implied. The subject who tells a self-story or personal experience story is, of course, at the center of the life that is told about. The researcher who reads and interprets a self-story is at the center of his or her interpretation of that story. Two interpretive structures thus interact. The two circles overlap to the degree that the researcher is able to live his or her way into the subject's personal experience stories and self-stories. These circles will never overlap completely, for the subject's experiences will never be those of the researcher.

Capturing the Phenomenon

Capturing the phenomenon involves locating and situating what is to be studied in the natural world. Deconstruction deals with what has been done with the phenomenon in the past. Capture deals with what the researcher is doing with the phenomenon in the present, in his or her study. Capture involves the following steps on the part of the researcher:

1. Securing multiple cases and personal histories that embody the phenomenon in question
2. Locating the crises and epiphanies of the lives of the persons being studied
3. Obtaining multiple personal experience stories and self-stories from the subjects in question concerning the topic or topics under investigation (Thompson, 1978)

Exemplars: Battered Wives, the Alcoholic

Cho (1987) collected personal experience st[ories] rean wives. She obtained her stories from women 64 battered Korean wives. She obtained her stories from women 64 battered Korean zation in Seoul, Korea, the Women's Hotline, wh[ich c]alled an organization battered wives from 10:00 a.m. to 6:00 p.m. on wee[kdays] and from 10:00 a.m. to 2:00 p.m. on Saturdays. Cho worked as a volu[nteer in] the organization. She took calls from battered wives on the hot line a[nd held] conversations with some of them concerning their battering exp[eriences.] From these conversations emerged the personal experience stories that sh[e an]alyzed in her study.

In my study of the alcoholic self, I went to the places where alcoholics gathered. I presented myself as a person interested in A.A. I have alcoholic family members. I formed friendships with recovering alcoholics and their spouses and children. I also became friends with alcoholism counselors and other treatment personnel in treatment centers. I was able to listen to alcoholics talking in their homes, in public places where they drank, in hospital emergency rooms where they went for medical treatment, in detoxification and treatment centers, and in A.A. meetings. The stories presented in Chapter 3 of the printer who went to A.A. and the 12-Step call are examples of the types of personal experience stories and interactions that I gathered in my study.

By capturing the phenomenon being studied, the researcher makes it available to the reader. The researcher presents experiences as they occur or as they have been reconstructed. When the researcher plans to group stories around a common theme, he or she must collect multiple stories. This allows the researcher to compare and contrast the stories of many different individuals located in different phases of the experience under investigation. Multiple stories allow the researcher to identify convergences in experience, although he or she can use any story if it contributes to a general understanding of the phenomenon. However, when a researcher uses a story, he or she must be sure it meets the criteria for interpreting biographical material discussed in Chapter 3.

Bracketing the Phenomenon

Bracketing is Husserl's (1913/1962, p. 86) term. In bracketing the phenomenon, the researcher holds the phenomenon up for serious inspection, taking it out of the world where it occurs. The researcher dissects the phenomenon, uncovering, defining, and analyzing its elements and essential structures. The researcher treats the phenomenon as a text or a document;

that is, as an instance of the phenomenon being studied. The researcher does not interpret the phenomenon in terms of the standard meanings given to it by the existing literature. Those are suspended and put aside during bracketing. In the deconstruction the researcher confronts the subject matter, as much as possible, bracketing, the researcher on its own terms.

Bracketing involves the following steps, which parallel two of the steps in interpretation discussed in Chapter 3 (subdividing the text into key experience units and analyzing each unit interpretively).

1. Locating within the personal experience story or self-story key phrases and statements that speak directly to the phenomenon in question

2. Interpreting the meanings of these phrases, as an informed reader

3. Obtaining the subject's interpretations of these phrases, if possible

4. Inspecting these meanings for what they reveal about the essential, recurring features of the phenomenon being studied

5. Offering a tentative statement about or definition of the phenomenon in terms of the essential recurring features identified in Step 4

Exemplars: The Balls Story, Battered Wives

Dolby-Stahl (1985) offers a bracketed interpretation of her mother's "balls" story (discussed in Chapter 3). She took the text of the story apart and interpreted key phrases. She then indicated how those phrases contributed to the essential, interpreted meaning of the story, both for her and for her mother.

Cho's interpretation of the stories of the Korean battered wives she interviewed focused on the importance of resentment (*ressentiment*; see Scheler, 1912/1961) in the Korean family. She based this interpretation on her bracketed reading of the personal experience narratives of the battered wives. This interpretation argued that there are seven stages to resentment once violence enters a marriage: craving for genuine conjugal love, rejection, feelings of hatred, feelings of revenge, repression of revenge, deep resentment, and secret craving for revenge. When a wife reaches the last of these stages, she harbors a desire to kill her husband. A wife speaks:

Until he comes back at night, I can't sleep, I can't eat, I can't rest. I hate and hate. . . . For 14 years of our marriage, this feeling has built up. My nerve is so weak that I take a pill to rest. . . . I just want to kill him. (quoted in Cho, 1987, p. 250)

Cho's bracketed reading of stories like this led her to develop the interpretation of resentment given above. Cho carefully defines each of the stages listed above (craving, rejection, hatred, and so on) in terms of actual statements made by the Korean wives.

Bracketing and Semiotics

One strategy that is useful in bracketing is semiotics, a technique for reading the meaning of words and signs within narrative and interactional texts (see Barthes, 1957/1972). A semiotic reading directs attention to oppositions and the key words and terms that organize a text. It suggests that these terms (signs) are organized by a code, or a system of larger meanings. These meanings are, in turn, organized in terms of oppositions. The full meaning of a text unfolds as it is told or read. A semiotic reading works from part to whole and from whole to part. It uncovers the codes that organize a text and examines the oppositions that structure its meaning. It draws attention to the multiple meanings of key words and utterances within interactional and narrative texts. It asks the analyst to perform both static and dynamic, or processual, readings of narratives.

A Semiotic Analysis of the Balls Story

Consider again the "balls" story told by Dolby-Stahl's (1985) mother. The larger code that gives the story meaning is the teller's position as a schoolteacher and a mother telling a story about something that happened one day at a country school in Indiana. Within this code are words and phrases (P.E. teacher, coach, basketball) that have specific meanings in the code (e.g., coaches have basketballs). The oppositions that exist in the story deal with (a) men goofing off and women working, (b) men's dirty talk and women's work talk, (c) dumb little things that can embarrass a person to death, and (d) things that aren't funny at the time that are later funny.

The key concept in the story revolves around the word *balls* ("great big basketballs") and the missing word *testicles*. The meaning of the word *balls* is complex. It emerges from within the story and includes balls rolling against the storyteller's door; her statement "What do you mean rolling your balls down the hall!?"; the men bursting out in laughter; and her being embarrassed, realizing that the word *balls* carries a double meaning.

This woman's story, like all personal experience narratives, is doubly complex: First, the experience as it was lived was both funny and embarrassing; second, the experience as told is again funny, but now, in the telling, the teller distances herself from the original experience. Hence the original semiotic meanings of the story are not the same as those contained in its retelling. The first time through, the meanings turned on the storyteller's being embarrassed. Experienced immediately after they occurred and in the retelling, they become funny.

Constructing the Phenomenon

Construction of the phenomenon builds on bracketing. In this stage, the researcher classifies, orders, and reassembles the phenomenon back into a coherent whole. If bracketing is taking something apart, constructing is putting it back together. Construction involves the following:

1. Listing the bracketed elements of the phenomenon
2. Ordering these elements as they occur within the process or experience
3. Indicating how each element affects and is related to every other element in the process being studied
4. Stating concisely how the structures and parts of the phenomenon cohere into a totality

Exemplar: Resentment in Violent Marriages

Cho (1987, p. 249) defined the seven features of resentment (ressentiment) in the violent marriage (identified above) and then contextualized them in the following way. She states that in the beginning

> the wife craves . . . love. . . . it is rejected by the husband's adultery. . . . the incidence of battering happens . . . [and the wife] begins to feel hatred toward the husband. . . . the hatred increases as the battering continues. She wants revenge. . . . the feelings of revenge are repressed. . . . ressentiment arises out of this situation. . . . her craving for revenge never stops. . . . the revenge plan . . . [she] has in mind is not to end the relationship . . . but to restore it with the punishment. (p. 262)

In this contextualizing statement, Cho creates a processual definition and interpretation of resentment in the violent marriage. She assembles the elements in a sequential manner, indicating how each builds on and influences the others.

The Goal of Construction

The researcher's goal in constructing the phenomenon is to re-create experience in terms of its constituent, analytic elements. In discussing the phenomenological study of emotion, Merleau-Ponty (1964) describes this process in the following words: "One gathers together the lived facts involv-

The following story is an example. The speaker is an alcoholic who has been sober and free of drugs for nearly 8 months. He is speaking to a group of A.A. members.

I used to drug and drink with my old friends. We'd picnic and party. One time it went on for 5 days over the 4th of July. Now I don't drink or drug anymore and its like we haven't got anything in common. I mean now that I'm in recovery, my recovery means more than anything else to me. So it's like I don't have these old friends anymore. I've only got friends in recovery now. I've got this customer. He tends bar. He keeps asking me to come by and have a drink. I can't tell him I'm an alcoholic and don't drink anymore. Its like I've lost this friend too. But man, I stand back and look at these people and look at me. It's like they're standin' still, goin' nowhere, and I'm movin' forward. They're back where I used to be. I'm glad I'm a recovering alcoholic and don't have to do that stuff anymore.

The meanings and effects of recovery for this person are given in the above statements. These meanings and effects are shaped by the language and practices of Alcoholics Anonymous. The speaker connects his recovery to the loss of old friends and the gaining of new ones. He connects his recovery as an alcoholic to his statements concerning where he is going and where his friends are. Meaning is given in his experiences.

Interpretive Criteria

Interpretive materials are evaluated in terms of the following criteria:

1. Do they illuminate the phenomenon as lived experience?
2. Are they based on thickly contextualized materials?
3. Are they historically and relationally grounded?
4. Are they processual and interactional?
5. Do they engulf what is known about the phenomenon?
6. Do they incorporate prior understandings of the phenomenon?
7. Do they cohere and produce understanding?
8. Are they unfinished?

Each of these questions requires brief discussion.

Illumination. An interpretation must illuminate or bring alive what is being studied. This can occur only when the interpretation is based on materials that come from the world of lived experience. Unless ordinary people speak, we cannot interpret their experiences.

Thickly contextualized materials. Interpretations are built up out of events and experiences that are described in detail. Thickly contextualized materials are dense. They record experience as it occurs. They locate experience in social situations. They record thoughts, meanings, emotions, and actions. They speak from the subject's point of view.

Historical and relational grounding. Interpretive materials must also be historical and relational. That is, they must unfold over time and they must record the significant social relationships that exist among the subjects being studied. Historically, or temporally, the materials must be presented as slices of ongoing interaction. They must also be located within lived history.

Process and interaction. These two dimensions should be clear. An interpretive account must be both processual and interactional. Each example that I have offered in the preceding three chapters has met this criterion.

Engulfment of what is known. Engulfing what is known about the phenomenon in question involves including all that is known to be relevant about it. This means that the interpreter must be an "informed reader" of the phenomenon, as I have argued in Chapter 3. Engulfing expands the framework for interpretation. It attempts to exclude nothing that would be relevant for the interpretation and understanding that is being formulated. Because understanding and interpretation are temporal processes, what is regarded as important at one point may at a later time be judged not to be central. Interpretation and understanding are always unfinished and incomplete (see below).

Prior understandings. Engulfing merges with the problem of incorporating prior understandings into the interpretation of a segment of experience. Prior understandings include background information and knowledge about the area of interest; concepts, hypotheses, and propositions contained in the research literature; and previously acquired information about subjects and their experiences. Nothing can be excluded, including how the researcher judged the phenomenon at the outset of an investigation. This is the case because the researcher's prior understandings shape what he or she sees, hears, writes about, and interprets. Hence prior understandings are part of what is interpreted. To exclude them is to risk biasing the interpretation in the direction of false objectivity.

Coherence and understanding. This criterion concerns whether the interpretation produces an understanding of the experience that coalesces into a coherent, meaningful whole. A coherent interpretation includes all relevant information and prior understandings. It is based on materials that are historical, relational, processual, and interactional. A coherent interpretation is based on thickly described materials. The reader is led through the interpretation in a meaningful way. The grounds for the interpretation are given, and the reader can decide whether to agree or disagree with the interpretation that is offered.

Unfinished interpretations. All interpretations are unfinished, provisional, and incomplete (Denzin, 1984a, p. 9). They start anew when the researcher returns to the phenomenon. This means that interpretation is always conducted from within the hermeneutic circle. As a researcher comes back to an experience and interprets it, his or her prior interpretations and understandings shape what he or she now sees and interprets. This does not mean that interpretation is inconclusive, for conclusions are always drawn. It only means that interpretation is never finished. To think otherwise is to foreclose one's interpretations before one begins. That is, an individual should not start a research project thinking that he or she will exhaust all that can be known about the phenomenon by the time the project is completed.

CONCLUSION

In this chapter I have discussed how interpretive researchers formulate their research questions and have shown how researchers conceptualize the phenomena to be studied within the worlds of lived experience. I have also presented the steps taken in interpretive research and the criteria for evaluating such research. Because the subject matter of interpretive studies is always biographical, the lives of ordinary men and women play a central role in the research texts that are created. Their lives and their problems are, after all, the phenomena that interpretive researchers study.

In a certain sense, interpretive researchers hope to understand their subjects better than the subjects understand themselves, to see effects and power where subjects see only emotion and personal meaning (Dilthey,

1900/1976, pp. 259-260). Often researchers form interpretations of their subjects' actions that the subjects themselves would not give. This is so because researchers are often in positions to see things that subjects cannot see. The full range of factors that play on individuals' experiences is seldom apparent to those individuals. Interpretive researchers have access to perspectives on subjects' lives that the subjects often lack. Such researchers also have methods of interpretation available to them that the subjects seldom have (Denzin, 1984a, p. 257). However, the interpretations that researchers develop about their subjects' lives must be understandable to the subjects. If they are not, they are unacceptable.

5

Situating Interpretation

Any study of consequential biographical experience must be located in the natural social world. This chapter examines the problems involved in situating an interpretive
study. The discussion extends the analysis of capturing the phenomenon under study
offered in Chapter 4. In capture, the researcher secures multiple cases and personal histories of persons who have experienced the problem or phenomenon being studied. The
researcher obtains personal experience stories and self-stories from these individuals
and interprets them.

Situating, or locating, an interpretation involves the following steps:

1. Determining when and where persons experiencing the phenomenon of
   interest come together and interact (the problems of timing, history, and
   mapping)
2. Gaining access to the setting
3. Learning the languages that are spoken and the meanings that are employed in these situations
4. Connecting individuals, biographies, and social types to the relevant situations of interaction

TIMING, HISTORY, AND MAPPING

The task of ethnography now becomes the unraveling of a conundrum:
what is the nature of locality, as a lived experience, in a globalized,
deterritorialized world? (Appadurai, 1991, p. 191)

Ethnography has gone local. The idea of the foreign, far-off field site to
which a researcher travels has been reconceptualized. The field of ethnography and " 'the field' of 'fieldwork' are thus politically and epistemologically interconnected" (Gupta & Ferguson, 1997, p. 3). As interpretive
researchers, we create the field of observation through our interpretive practices. The field is where we are.

Appadurai (1996) contends that the local always bears traces of the global. He uses the term *ethnoscapes* to refer to global flows of people and the "changing social, territorial, and cultural reproduction of group identity in the late 20th century" (p. 48; see also McCall, 2001, p. 50). Thus does the *ethno* in ethnography become slippery, for the landscapes of group identity are no longer firmly planted in a single geographic site. Further, in the present global economy, commodities, including identities, easily cross borders and circulate and interact in cyberspace.

Indeed, interpretive ethnographers now understand that the intensively focused-upon single case or site has become a thing of the past. Marcus (1998) suggests that ethnographies should be conceptualized within a "multi-sited imaginary that provides the special context of significance and argument for the ethnography" (p. 14). Marcus suggests that such multi-sited research presents new challenges to "both ways of writing ethnography and ways of pursuing fieldwork. Within a multi-sited imaginary, tracing and describing the connections and relationships among sites previously thought incommensurate is ethnography's way of making arguments and providing its own contexts of significance" (p. 14). Beyond specific sites, "there is still ethnography all the way up and down rather than *only* the system" (p. 14).

Doing ethnography "all the way up and down" collapses the distinctions between micro and macro, between local and global (Abu-Lughod, 2001, p. 264). Single-site studies dissolve into multisited mobile ethnographies (Marcus, 1998, pp. 79-80). Thick ethnographic description of television audiences, for example, "requires a multisited ethnography wherein, as George Marcus has put it regarding commodities in a world system, one can follow the thing" (Abu-Lughod, 1997, p. 114).

Abu-Lughod (1997) describes her multisited feminist ethnography of television. For a period of time, she watched a television serial, *Mothers in the House of Love,* with a group of women from an Upper Egyptian village. The serial, produced in Cairo by urban professionals, was written by Fathiyya al-'Assal, a woman active in the Egyptian leftist party. Of her ethnography, Abu-Lughod (1997) states: "The relevant system here is national. Therefore I will start with the villagers, and their responses to the television serial. . . . But I also want to keep tracing the serial back to Cairo. . . . This approach will . . . allow us some insight into the dynamics of 'culture' " (p. 114). Stitched through her ethnography are conversations with Zaynab, a friend of a friend, whose household had been the friend's haven, and statements by al-'Assal in which she describes her goals in writing the television serial. Al-'Assal states:

I wanted to create a new role for older women. . . . I am sixty years old now. In the past when a woman was sixty she was supposed to sit at home waiting to die, having already married off her children. I now have four children and eight grandchildren, but because I have my own concerns and ambitions as a writer and a politician, I do not feel that I am getting older. I wanted to communicate this in a serial. (p. 117)

Temporal Mapping

The researcher must connect persons to situations. This process, which I call temporal mapping, involves two interrelated steps: (a) determining the temporal sequencing and organization of actions in the setting and (b) locating settings and persons in space (i.e., Where are these interactional situations located?). Any social structure is made up of interacting individuals who come together in social situations. Persons bring and experience their personal troubles in such situations. In these settings, people tell stories about personal troubles. These stories constitute the materials for interpretive studies.

Temporal mapping focuses on *who* does *what* with *whom, when,* and *where.* For example, the battered wives in Cho's Korean study came from middle-class marriages (the *who*). They called in to the Seoul hot line and told their stories to professional workers between the hours of 10:00 a.m. and 6:00 p.m. on weekdays and 10:00 a.m. and 2:00 p.m. on Saturdays. (Here the *what* becomes storytelling; the *with whom,* the professional listeners; and the *when* and *where,* the hours and places just indicated.)

The process of mapping is important for several reasons. First, unless the researcher knows how the processes to be studied are distributed through the social structure, in a multisited way, he or she risks studying atypical or unrepresentative instances of the phenomenon. Second, mapping builds a historical dimension into the research act. Every individual studied has a historical, biographical relationship to the event, crisis, or problem under investigation. (Mapping, in this sense, involves connecting individuals to situations. I discuss this below under the topic of mapping individuals.) Third, the sites that are studied (e.g., group meeting places, telephone hot lines, places of work, violent homes, clinics) have their own histories within the social structure. These histories have two dimensions: First, sites have histories with other sites (see the discussion below); second, sites have their own histories (when they were established and so on).

The fourth reason temporal mapping is important involves biography and personal experience. Temporal mapping is a process that every person, including the researcher, has to go through. Alcoholics and battered women, for example, have to learn when and where the interactions in which they participate take place. A battered woman can't call a hot line unless she knows the hours it operates. An alcoholic can't tell her story to an A.A. group unless she knows when and where a meeting is taking place. A researcher who is learning his or her way into and through a particular social structure will have experiences similar to those of a battered wife who is seeking help for the first time. This is part of the process of living one's way into the phenomenon being interpreted.

Exemplars

In my A.A. study, there were old groups (started in the 1960s) and new groups (started in the 1980s). New groups took on ways of interacting from old groups. Indeed, in some cases, new groups were started by persons from the old groups. Personal experience stories told in new groups were shaped, in part, by the customs and traditions established nearly 30 years ago in the original A.A. groups in the community. I would not have known this if I had not studied the historical relationships between sites.

The second important historical dimension of a site is its history within the local social structure. Cho (1987) notes that the Women's Hotline in Seoul, Korea, was established in 1983. It was the first such hot line for battered women in that city. Hence women who told their stories of battering to someone answering a hot line did so for the first time to the workers in this agency. When a new site for dealing with personal troubles opens up in a social structure, it receives stories that it will not receive later, when additional sites make their appearance. The telling of stories is shaped by the sites the social structure makes available for their telling.

Going Cyber

Consider the following two statements. They were made by newcomers to an Internet news-discussion group called alt.recovery.codependency (a.r.c.), an on-line newsgroup that draws on the tenets of the adult children of alcoholics (ACOA) movement and Co-Dependents Anonymous (CODA). Alt.recovery.codependency is one of many thousands of discussion groups that can be found on the Internet; these newsgroups form what is commonly called the usenet. The Internet users who participate in these discussion groups post messages that are disseminated to all the Internet sites carrying the newsgroups. Some users may respond to particular messages, creating "threads" or connected series of messages; still others may read posted messages without responding (this is called lurking; see Denzin, 1998, 1999a).

The internet is where my problems blossomed, and maybe with other avenues, it can be where I find some healing. (new male reader/member, a.r.c., September 5, 1996)

On my first visit to this newsgroup (a.r.c.), it was so wonderful to read about the work of your recovery and the joy of it. As I am just at the beginning of the self discovery and the hard work, I really thank you for sharing that. (new female reader/member, a.r.c., September 1, 1996)

The ethnoscapes of recovery have gone cyber and global, as these stories reveal. Recovery now takes on new meaning, and the effects of the recovery discourse are now played out in a new multisited space, all the way up and down the line, to paraphrase George Marcus.

Gaining Access and the Stages to Temporal Mapping

Temporal mapping, which necessarily merges with gaining access, requires the researcher to go through the following stages. By doing so, the researcher implements the processes of capturing the phenomenon (discussed in Chapter 4) and locating the subject (briefly discussed in Chapter 3):

1. Identifying the institutional sites where troubles are brought
2. Developing an explanation concerning one's desire to be present in these sites and to study the interaction and experiences that go on within them (see Adler & Adler, 1987, pp. 39-43)
3. Enumerating these sites, obtaining their addresses, and determining the timetables that structure interaction in the sites
4. Writing, as much as possible in this early stage, the history of the sites and their relation (historical and interactional) to other sites
5. Determining who routinely comes to the sites
6. Securing personal histories from established persons in the sites
7. Beginning the process of listening for and collecting personal and self-stories concerning crises and epiphanies from the persons in the sites
8. Asking and refining the research question on a continual basis (which involves asking and listening for "how" answers to the ways that the problem in question was and continues to be a personal trouble for the individuals and groups being studied)

Exemplars: Battered Wives, Alcoholic Selves

In Chapter 4, I discussed how Cho (1987) obtained her materials on battered wives in Seoul, Korea. She followed the eight steps outlined above.

Her site was the Women's Hotline. Early in her study, she wrote a history of this facility and determined who was using it. She obtained personal histories from the founders of the agency and started collecting personal experience stories in her capacity as a telephone volunteer. She gained access to the setting (its hours were 10:00 a.m. to 6:00 p.m. on weekdays and 10:00 a.m. to 2:00 p.m. on Saturday) by immediately offering to work 7 days a week, from 9:00 a.m. to 7:00 p.m., doing secretarial chores, including proofreading, serving coffee and fruit to the workers, and assisting in the preparation of case stories for newspaper columns. Within a month, she had become a staff member in the organization.

In my study of A.A. on-line, I lurked. I was an unannounced reader of the postings on the usenet groups. In my community A.A. study, I went to the places where alcoholics and their families routinely gathered, including "open" A.A. meetings, which are open to anyone who has an interest in A.A. My research question, as noted in Chapter 3, involved "how ordinary men and women experience active alcoholism and recovery." I collected personal experience stories and self-stories involving these two sides of the alcoholic's experience.

I addressed the problems and steps involved in temporal mapping in the following ways. At one of the first meetings I attended, I obtained a listing of all the A.A. meetings in the community. This listing gave the names of the groups, the times that they met, and the addresses of the meeting places. There were more than 40 meetings a week, held either at noon or at 8:00 p.m. I then started attending meetings. Over the course of 3 months, I was able to go to every meeting on the original list. Because A.A. members often go to three or more meetings a week, I soon found myself in different meetings with people I had met at other meetings. I became known as a person who went to many meetings.

I started to meet persons who helped get A.A. started in the community in the early 1960s. These persons were chairing meetings I attended. I had coffee with them. They talked about A.A.'s early beginnings and told me when various groups first began to meet. These persons gave me histories of all the various A.A. groups. They also told me who went to which meetings, who was having problems staying sober, who was doing well, and so on.

While I was gathering this information, I was learning how to listen to A.A. stories. I began collecting personal experience stories and self-stories from members as they spoke at various meetings. I also listened to recovery stories told after A.A. meetings, when members went to local restaurants for coffee and dessert. In these ways I formed a working picture of the social structure of A.A. in the local community.

LEARNING THE
LANGUAGE AND ITS MEANINGS

As the researcher works his or her way into the research setting, the problems of language and meaning become important. Every group develops its own idiolect (Barthes, 1967) or special language. This language contains terms that are not commonly used and concepts that are not commonly understood in other groups. It attaches special meanings to what other groups perceive as everyday words. It also contains a code, or a set of rules for putting words together. The language, in this sense, will have an institutional and historical heritage that the researcher must uncover. Because each group is a distinct language community, the researcher must begin by learning the language that is spoken.

Steps to Learning a Language

Learning a language involves the following steps:

1. Isolating the key recurring terms used in the setting
2. Identifying how these terms are used by different social types in the setting (e.g., novices, newcomers, and old-timers; men and women)
3. Locating key printed and oral cultural texts that use these terms
4. Isolating differences in meanings and usage of terms by site, gender, and length of time in the social structure and culture of the group
5. Collecting stories and statements that contain these terms
6. Connecting these terms to personal experience, showing how their meanings and uses structure experience

Learning a language takes time (see the discussion below).

Language and the Process of Understanding

Language structures and creates the processes of understanding and interpretation. As I have noted in Chapter 2, interpretation sets forth the meaning of an event, statement, or process. In understanding, a person grasps the meaning of what has been interpreted. Understanding and interpretation are emotional processes. They involve shared experience and shared meanings. Experiences cannot be shared if the language and the meanings that organize the experiences are not understood. Shared linguistic understandings allow persons to construct common pasts and projected futures

(Couch, 1984, p. 1). When people share a language and its meanings, they can also share mutual understandings. This is the case because they can organize interactions that call forth in others common meanings attached to particular terms (see Perinbanayagam, 1985). These terms and their meanings, in turn, allow for the production of shared, meaningful experiences.

Exemplar: A.A.'s Language

In conducting my A.A. study, I had to learn a new language. I followed the steps outlined above. I isolated key terms, began to note how different types of A.A. members used those terms, began reading A.A.'s basic literature (the Big Book and *Twelve Steps and Twelve Traditions*; Alcoholics Anonymous World Services, 1976, 1953/1989), noted differences in the usage of the A.A. language among different members, collected stories that used the language, and began to study how this language was connected to ongoing personal experience.

A.A. is a distinct linguistic community. It makes use of special terms, codes, and meanings that are not immediately understandable to outsiders. Here are some examples: *bottom, Dr. Bob, "How It Works," "home group," GSR,* and *12&12.* When I first started attending meetings, I did not know what these terms meant. I later learned that *bottom* refers to falling so low in life that one became ready to accept A.A. I learned that Dr. Bob was the cofounder of A.A. (Dr. Robert Smith), that "How It Works" refers to the reading of A.A.'s 12 Steps at the beginning of a meeting, that a GSR is a group service representative, and that 12&12 is short for *The Twelve Steps and the Twelve Traditions.* Some of these terms are defined in the A.A. literature; others are part of A.A. folklore and must be learned from A.A. members, either directly or by listening to them talk. I learned what these terms meant by reading the A.A. literature (Denzin, 1987a) and by listening to members talk in meetings. Without an understanding of them, I could not have interpreted what members were saying when they told their stories at meetings. Lacking this understanding, I could not have participated in the shared A.A. experience (see the discussion below).

Novices, Newcomers, and Old-Timers

As A.A. gets inside the self of the alcoholic, the terms of the A.A. language become part of his or her A.A. vocabulary. As a member learns the A.A. language, he or she becomes part of the A.A. social structure. In A.A., there are at least four stages of language usage, reflecting length of membership; language usage differs depending on whether members are novices (persons just exposed to A.A.), newcomers (persons who have recently made a commitment to become members), regulars (persons who have been coming at least a year), or old-timers (those with more than 10 years of membership). Following are examples of the language of a novice, a newcomer, and an old-timer.

Novice

Consider the following self-story told by an alcoholic in a treatment center. He is speaking to his counselor about the A.A. Steps:

> What in the hell is a Step!? Hell I can't even remember the numbers. How do I take the damned things? How long does it take? When do I know I'm done? What's a _____ program? What do all these words mean? How can I meditate if I don't know what it means? What's a higher power? What's a defect of character? How do I make an amend? Christ I don't get any of this _____! _____ what do I do? Help me. (30-year-old salesman, in treatment for the first time)

This speaker evidences only a slight understanding of A.A. language. He does not know what *step, program, meditation, higher power, defect of character,* or *amend* mean. Not knowing the taken-for-granted meanings of these terms, he is unable to apply them to his own experience. If he becomes a member of A.A., he will, over the course of time, learn what these terms mean. He will also begin to feel comfortable with them.

Newcomer

Compare the preceding statement to the following, made by a man who has been in A.A. for 7 months:

> I read that story in the Big Book, "The Vicious Circle." That's me. I get sober a few days, then I drink and I can't stop. I've been here 7 months and I have 3 months' sobriety. I just couldn't stay stopped. Always something. Boss would yell at me. My mother'd be sick. The car wouldn't start. Green Bay would lose a football game. Any damned excuse to go off and get drunk. I just about lost my good job. Today the boss is happy with me and everything's goin' good. I finally got a sponsor and got me a regular set of meetings I go to. It's working for me. Last night, though, I wanted to drink. My sister called and told me I was a quitter for stopping drinking. She's an alcoholic too. It scares her that I've quit. She wants me to keep drinking. Three months ago I would have gone out and drank a fifth over that call.

Today I don't need ... year-old mechanic, single; field conversation,
January 10, 1985)

This man is at a F... tep Meeting. He is speaking to a novice who is at her
first meeting. Se... months earlier, this speaker was a novice. He has now
learned how to ... his story, and he tells it as suggested in A.A.'s Big Book
(Acoholics A...nymous World Services, 1976).

Old-Timer

Here is a speaker who had been in A.A. for more than 30 years when he
died at the age of 76. He takes the framework for his story from A.A.'s Big
Book, which contains 44 life stories organized in terms of the following
statement: "Our stories disclose in a general way what we used to be like,
what happened, and what we are like now."

Bill Wilson could have told my story. Same circumstances. Bright prospects for a prominent career in business. Good school, loving parents,
lovely wife, nice home. Everything. Heavy social drinking in the early
days. The good life. But the drinking got heavier. I was taking a bottle to
work in my briefcase. Nips in the morning to get started. Early lunches so I
could get a fix before I started to shake too much. Then I started getting
home late from work. I'd stop for a few and a few would turn into all night. I
became irresponsible toward my family.
    I decided I needed to switch jobs. So I did and for a while it was better.
Then I started hitting the bottle more and more. Some days I'd leave at
noon. Sometimes I'd call in sick on Monday. It got so I couldn't go longer
than an hour without a drink. The wife left me and took the kids. I said, "To
hell with them," and I took an expensive apartment in the city. Tried to live
the bachelor life. Started ending up in the drunk tanks. Went into a sanatorium to dry out. Got drunk the day I got out. That was in the early 40s. People were talking about this A.A. thing at the sanatorium. I read that Jack
Alexander article. A friend got a copy of the Big Book and gave it to me. I
looked at it and threw it away.
    Kept on drinking. I finally lost my job, everything. Another place to dry
out but this time when I came out I was ready to stop. I got to an A.A. meeting and saw that Big Book. This time I read it. It fit me to a T. They said
there was hope if I followed their simple program. I started going to meetings. Got a sponsor. Dried out, got sober. Got my old job back, and after a
year the wife and kids came back. I've been in ever since. I owe everything
to A.A. and to Bill Wilson, Dr. Sam Shoemaker, Dr. Bob, and all those
old-timers who held in there and kept A.A. going. In the early days we used
to drive 500 miles a week just to make meetings every night. There weren't

many then, you know. We all hung together and helped each other. Just like you people are today. (field observation, May 2, 1982)

Several points may be taken from these three stories. The third speaker presumes a knowledge of who Bill Wilson (the cofounder of A.A.) was. The second and third speakers assume a knowledge of the Big Book. Because Wilson virtually wrote the Big Book, when each man uses these two-word phrases he locates himself within the taken-for-granted history of A.A. The third speaker in fact identifies himself with Wilson in terms of the bright prospects of his business career, good school, loving parents, and so forth. He becomes Wilson as he talks. Indeed, as he tells his story he tells a version of A.A.'s story in the United States. He thus draws his listeners into a central part of A.A.'s folklore.

The third speaker makes reference to A.A.'s simple program. The word *program* glosses, or includes, A.A.'s 12 Steps and 12 Traditions. It also includes A.A.'s spiritual program, which involves a higher power, daily meditation and prayer, the Serenity Prayer, the Fourth and Fifth Steps, carrying the message, and so on. The first speaker lacks an understanding of all of these terms. In short, by using the word *program,* the third man creates for his listeners a chain of meanings and associations that range across all of the A.A. Steps and Traditions. The word *program* glosses all of these associations and meanings.

The third speaker's text is filled with A.A. history and the special meanings contained in the A.A. language. The second speaker, with only 7 months in A.A., evidences a similar understanding of how the A.A. language works. His story also contains other references to the A.A. language, including terms such as *sobriety* (not drinking and working the program) and *sponsor* (an A.A. member who helps another individual stay sober and work the program).

Interpreting Language

As a linguistic process, interpretation involves both learning the language that is to be interpreted and learning how to interpret that language once one has learned it. This is the point of the example above of the novice's asking his counselor about the 12 Steps. This man has yet to learn the language that he is being asked to apply to himself. As a result, he cannot interpret what that language will do for him. More is involved. Learning how to interpret a language requires that one examine how that language is employed by the speaker in question. It requires a historical understanding of the language, the speaker, and the audience he or she is speaking to. It requires an understanding of the range of meanings a speaker might intend when he or she uses particular terms.

When a person learns a language and then puts it into use, the language begins to structure that person's experiences. Language, in this sense, speaks for the speaker. It gives the speaker a set of terms that convey and capture meaningful experience in ways that other terms could not. This is what the A.A. novice salesman is struggling with. He does not know how to fit A.A.'s language to his experience. As a result, he cannot interpret his experience. He has come up against a wall and is asking for help.

Interpretive methodologists must learn and grasp this double structure that is embedded in language. They must learn the language that is spoken by those they study. They must then learn the possible uses to which that language can be put. In addition, they must learn how to read and decode that language once it takes the shape of a social text that is given in self-stories. Language, in this respect, is the gateway to the inner interpretive structures of the lives that are being studied.

RESEARCHER AS NEWCOMER
AND THE KNOWING SUBJECT

Not everybody uses or understands language in the same ways. This is the point of the examples I have given above of the three different types of speakers of the A.A. language: the novice, the newcomer, and the old-timer. The second step in learning a language (as indicated above) involves determining how different types of people in the research site use the language. This requires that the researcher identify two interrelated elements: (a) the different social types in the site and (b) the connection of individuals and biographies to situations of interaction. In this phase of situating interpretation, the researcher begins to classify and categorize biographical information.

The researcher is like the A.A. newcomer. He or she must learn how to map a social structure in order to connect individuals to situations. Like the newcomer, the investigator must learn a new language and learn how to apply that language to personal experience.

The researcher seeks to become a knowledgeable member of the social structure being studied. He or she seeks to know what the typical member of the group knows, but more as well: The researcher wants to know everything that is relevant, so that he or she can formulate thick interpretations of personal experience stories. This means the researcher wants to be an all-knowing subject in the situation. Is this possible? Is there ever an all-knowing subject, or a person who knows everything that is relevant in a situation? The answer, of course, is no. Critical theorists such as Habermas, Marcuse, Adorno, and Horkheimer (see Bottomore, 1984; Kincheloe & McLaren, 2000) have discussed this problem and have argued for the creation of social structures in which meaningful, undistorted human communication can occur. In such social structures knowing subjects would exist, for individuals would have access to and understand the forces that shape and impinge upon their experiences.

An all-knowing subject is a fiction. The best that the researcher can hope for is to find reflective subjects who can tell their stories and the stories of others. The researcher, like the subject, is always in the hermeneutic circle, always seeing situations and structures in terms of prior understandings and prior interpretations. Full, objective, all-encompassing knowledge of a subject or a situation is never possible. I will take up this problem in greater detail in later chapters.

CONCLUSION

In this chapter I have described the four steps a researcher must take in situating an interpretive study. I have argued that it is seldom possible to do a single-sited ethnography. In the current world system, ethnographies have become multisited. Mobile ethnographers follow their mobile subjects in and through everyday reality as well as into the newsgroups of cyberspace. In doing a multisited ethnography, the researcher must address the problems of temporal mapping, gaining access to settings, learning a language, and connecting individuals, biographies, and social types to situations of interaction. I have offered examples from several different research sites, and I have likened the researcher to a newcomer in a social group.

Interpretive researchers examine how social groups and social structures create the conditions for the experiencing and expression of personal troubles. The discussion thus comes full circle. The original research site, whether it is an A.A. meeting, a usenet group in cyberspace, or a hot line for victims of domestic abuse, must always be seen in terms of the histories that stand behind that social structure. In this chapter I have discussed the members who make up the structure in terms of social types. These social types, in turn, have their own histories, located in the biographies of other group members. The interpretive study once again becomes historical as it attempts to interpret the relationships among individuals, turning-point social experiences, personal experience stories, and social groups.

6

Thick Description

This chapter addresses the topic of thick description. Description is the art of giving an account of something in words. In interpretive studies, thick descriptions and inscriptions are deep, dense, detailed accounts of problematic experiences. These accounts often state the intentions and meanings that organize actions. Thin descriptions, in contrast, lack detail and simply report facts. They are also called glosses. This chapter compares these forms of description, giving examples of both types and specifying their relationships to thick interpretation.

A DOUBLE CRISIS

The narrative and performative turn in the human disciplines, as I have argued in Chapter 1, makes problematic two key assumptions of interpretive research. The first is that qualitative researchers can directly capture lived experience. Such experience, it is now argued, is created in the social text written by the researcher. This is the representational crisis. It confronts the inescapable problem of representation, but does so within a framework that makes the direct link between experience and text problematic.

The second assumption makes the traditional criteria for evaluating interpretive qualitative research problematic. This is the legitimation crisis. It involves a serious rethinking of such concepts as validity, generalizability, and reliability—concepts already retheorized in feminist and interpretive discourses. It is now understood that social scientists are not aloof, objective observers of cultures and their processes. Rather, social scientists write culture; they create culture through the process of writing. Writing is an interpretive act. Researchers do not describe culture; rather, they *inscribe* it, to use Patti Lather's (1991) term.

Accordingly, thick descriptions can no longer be treated as privileged documents. These protracted, microscopic ethnographic descriptions, as Geertz (1973b) reminds us, are interpretations of interpretations, conventionalized ways of bringing the world into play. They do not present the world as it is; rather, they create the world. In so doing, they "present the sociological mind with bodied stuff on which to feed" (Geertz, 1973b, p. 23; see also Abu-Lughod, 1997, p. 113).

Thick description is a basic feature of interpretive ethnography. Such work always pays attention to the "contingent ways in which all social categories emerge, become naturalized, and intersect in people's conception of themselves and their world" (Rofel, 1994, p. 703). These categories are produced through and in everyday practices, practices that are "enmeshed within other social fields of meaning and power" (Rofel, 1994, p. 703).

Abu-Lughod (1997) discusses the need for thick descriptions in media studies, noting that there is considerable "thinness" in many studies of popular culture. We must, she says, "return to the insights of Geertz's 'Thick Description.' . . . We need to do ethnographies of production . . . [while] tracing the enmeshment of television in other social fields. . . . the key is to experiment with ways of placing television more seamlessly within the sort of rich social and cultural context that has been our ideal since . . . Malinowski. . . . [We need] thick descriptions of social discourses in particular places" (pp. 112-113).

In describing her project, Abu-Lughod (1997) argues that thick descriptions of television "can be made to speak to big words. . . . To write about television in Egypt . . . is to write about the articulation of the transnational, the national, the local and the personal. . . . Working on television enables more local intervention. . . . through my thick descriptions . . . I can begin to tease apart the structures of power within which subaltern groups live their lives and the ways television is a new part of that" (p. 128). This work allows her to enter into debates with Egyptian writers, intellectuals, and politicians concerning the social problems facing ordinary people and the unrealistic, often patronizing, modernist solutions television seems to offer for these problems. Thus can thick description quickly take on political implications.

THICK DESCRIPTION AS
PERFORMATIVE WRITING

Interpretive interactionism seeks to bring lived experience before the reader. A major goal of the interpretive writer is to create a text that permits a willing reader to share vicariously in the experiences that have been captured. When this occurs, the reader can naturalistically generalize (Stake, 1978, p. 5) his or her experiences to those that have been captured. This is what thick description does. It is a form of performative writing. It creates verisimilitude, a space for the reader to imagine his or her way into the life experiences of another. Thick descriptions capture and record the voices of lived experience, or the "prose of the world" (Merleau-Ponty, 1973). Thick description contextualizes experience. It is interpretation, and it contains the necessary ingredients for thick interpretation, the topic of the next chapter.

As a realistic and naturalistic form of performative writing, a thick description, as noted in Chapter 2, does more than record what a person is doing. It goes beyond mere fact and surface appearances. It presents detail, context, emotion, and the webs of social relationships that join persons to one another. It enacts what it describes. Thick description evokes emotionality and self-feelings. It inserts history into experience. It establishes the significance of an experience or sequence of events for the person or persons in question. In thick description the voices, feelings, actions, and meanings of interacting individuals are heard, made visible. Performance texts flow from thick descriptions; an example is Mrs. Anderson's description of the night the school board voted to desegregate, as presented in Chapter 2.

Thick descriptions are implemented through the use what Richardson (2000) refers to as "creative analytic practice." As discussed in Chapter 3, this includes first-person narratives, poetry, performance texts, fiction stories, literary nonfiction, layered accounts, writing-stories, responsive readings, personal memoirs, and cultural criticism.

THICK DESCRIPTION-AS-INSCRIPTION

Thick inscription creates verisimilitude—that is, the realistic description produces for readers the feeling that they have experienced, or could experience, the events being described. There are several different types of thick description-as-inscription. Below, I examine these types and compare them to the different forms of thin description. I take up the following topics: (a) exemplars of thick description, (b) types and examples of thin description, (c) types of thick description, (d) good and bad thick description, and (e) the relations among description, inscription, and interpretation.

Thick description may be defined, in part, by its contrast to thin description. Ryle (1968) provides an example of thin description:

> You hear someone come out with "Today is the third of February." What is he doing? Obviously the thinnest possible description of what he was doing would fit a gramophone equally well, that he was launching this sequence of syllables into the air. (pp. 8-9)

This is a thin description or inscription of a person making a statement. It lacks detail and density. I have given numerous examples of thick description in the preceding chapters (recall Mrs. Anderson's memories); in addition, consider the following.

Exemplars

Torture as a Public Spectacle

Foucault opens his book *Discipline and Punish: The Birth of the Prison* (1979) with the following thick description of the public torture of a man who had attempted to assassinate King Louis XV of France:

> On 2 March 1757 Damiens the regicide was condemned "to make the *amende honorable* before the main door of the Church of Paris," where he was to be "taken and conveyed in a cart, wearing nothing but a shirt, holding a torch of burning wax weighing two pounds" . . . where, on a scaffold . . . the flesh will be torn from his breasts, arms, thighs and calves with red-hot pincers . . . then his body drawn and quartered by four horses and his limbs and body consumed by fire, reduced to ashes and his ashes thrown to the winds. An officer of the watch left this account of the event: the executioner, his sleeves rolled up, took the steel pincers . . . and pulled first at the calf of the right leg, then at the thigh . . . then at the breasts. . . . Damiens . . . cried out . . . "Pardon, Lord." (p. 4)

This is a thick inscription that re-creates a historical situation, the public torture and execution of an attempted assassin. It goes beyond a thin account of the execution, which might have simply stated that on March 2, 1757, Damiens, who had attempted to kill the king of France, was executed. (Foucault's presentation of this case goes on for several pages.)

Ways of the Hand

Phenomenologist David Sudnow (1978) describes the movement of his hands across the piano keyboard as he learns to play jazz:

> Sitting at the piano and moving into the production of a chord, the chord as a whole was prepared for as the hand moved toward the keyboard, and the terrain was seen as a field relative to the task. . . .
>   There was chord A and chord B, separated from one another. . . . A's production entailed a tightly compressed hand, and B's . . . an open and extended spread. . . . The beginner gets from A to B disjointedly. (pp. 9-10)

This is a close-up representation of the movements of the hand as it attempts to find its proper places on the piano keyboard. A thin description might have stated, "I had trouble learning the piano keyboard." In the next excerpt, Sudnow describes himself some months later, playing before a group of friends:

> The Music was not mine. It was going on all around me. I was in the midst of the music. . . . I was up there trying to do this jazz I practiced nearly all day. . . . I was on a bucking bronco of my body's doings. . . . between the chord-changing beating of the left hand at more or less "regular intervals" according to the chart, the melody movements of the right, and the rather more smoothly managed and securely pulsing background of the bass player and drummer, there obtained the most mutually alienative relations. (p. 30)

In this excerpt Sudnow is interpreting as he describes his body's attempts to play jazz. He is looking down at his own conduct, describing his feelings and his actions at the same time. This description is different from the first, in which he depicts only actions.

Running From a Cockfight

Anthropologist Clifford Geertz (1973a) describes how he and his wife ran away from a Balinese cockfight:

> A truck full of policemen armed with machine guns roared up. Amid great screeching cries of "pulisi! pulisi!" from the crowd, the policemen jumped out. . . . People raced down the road, disappeared headfirst over walls. . . . my wife and I decided . . . that the thing to do was run too. We ran down the main village street. . . . About halfway down another fugitive ducked suddenly into a compound—his own . . . —and we . . . followed him. . . . his wife, who had . . . been through this sort of thing before, whipped out a table, a tablecloth, three chairs, and three cups of tea, and we all . . . sat down . . . and sought to compose ourselves. (pp. 414-415)

Geertz, like Sudnow in the example above, interprets as he describes. A thin description might have stated simply, "My wife and I ran when the police came, and we ended up having tea with a native couple."

THIN DESCRIPTION-AS-INSCRIPTION

I turn next to the characteristics of thin description. As the quote from Ryle (1968) above indicates, thin descriptions simply report facts or occurrences. More is involved in such descriptions, however. Thin descriptions and interpretations abound in the social sciences. They find their expression in correlation coefficients, path diagrams, F ratios, dummy variables, structural equations, statistical tests of significance, and social indicators. They are also present in certain forms of qualitative research, in which investigators slight description in the rush to code, do content analysis, and formulate interpretations. Indeed, a great deal of interpretive theory in the social sciences is based on thinly described materials. The result has been too much theory and not enough description. David Sudnow's (1978) study of his piano-playing experiences, as he learned how to improvise at the keyboard, represents the kind of careful mixture and balance of thick description and thick interpretation that I am advocating.

Thin Descriptions and Types of Words

Thin descriptions gloss events; that is, they give superficial, partial, and sparse accounts. They use few words to describe complex, meaningful events. They often let big words, often social science terms and concepts, do the work of many little words. Thin descriptions do not present lived experience.

In thin descriptions researchers often use second-order, experience-distant, social science words instead of first-order, experience-near concepts and terms (Geertz, 1983, pp. 57-58; Schutz, 1964). An experience-near concept is one that "someone—a patient, a subject—in our case an informant—might . . . naturally . . . use to define what he or his fellows see, feel, think, imagine, and so on" (Geertz, 1983, p. 57). An experience-distant concept "is one that specialists . . . an experimenter, an ethnographer . . . employ to forward their scientific . . . aims. . . . 'Love' is an experience-near concept, 'object cathexis' is an experience-distant one" (Geertz, 1983, p. 57). Experience-near concepts come from everyday language. Experience-distant concepts come from social science theories. Thin descriptions use experience-distant concepts. Thick descriptions employ experience-near concepts.

Types of Thin Description

There are four basic types of thin description. The first type, everyday glosses, are found in descriptions given by non-social scientists.

Everyday Glosses

Everyday interactants often gloss, or give only partial accounts of, their actions and experiences (Garfinkel, 1967, pp. 4-5, 20-21). These descriptions permit individuals "to conduct their conversational affairs without interference" (Garfinkel, 1967. p. 42). Garfinkel (1967) offers an example:

> My friend and I were talking about a man whose overbearing attitude annoyed us. My friend expressed his feeling.
> (S) I'm sick of him.
> (E) Would you explain what is wrong with you that you are sick?
> (S) Are you kidding? You know what I mean.
> (E) Please explain your ailment.
> (S) (He listened to me with a puzzled look.) What came over you? We never talk this way, do we? (p. 44)

When persons are challenged about the meanings of glossed words (e.g., "I'm sick of him"), they may react with alarm, for they assume that others "know" what they mean by their talk.

Social Science Glosses

The next three types of thin description are found in the work of social scientists. The first occurs in those situations where researchers slight description in order to give thick, detailed, theoretical accounts of events or processes. The second occurs when investigators have collected thick descriptions but then compress those materials into summary statements, often using social theory words. In both cases, the researchers use experience-distant, second-order terms. The third type of thin description occurs when an author offers a typified thick description, describing an ideal case but not actual experience. The result is thinly described experience.

Exemplars

Courtship Violence—Thick Theory, Thin Description

Sociologist Randall Collins (1975) describes (and interprets) the dating system as it works in American youth culture. Force and violence (rape) are basic features of this system:

> A mild use of force is taken into account in the dating system; women generally allow themselves to be made subject to force only after a tentative bargain has been struck.... The dating system developed ... just preceding World War I.... By 1937 Willard Waller had given his analysis of the "rating and dating complex" as a system in which marriageable young men and women tried to make erotic conquests and at the same time sorted themselves out into ranks of desirability ... culminating in marriage. (p. 251)

This lengthy statement glosses and compresses, through the use of terms like "rating and dating complex," significant social experiences. These experiences include rape and violence as part of dating and becoming married. There is no lived experience in this description of the American dating system.

Interaction in Small Groups

In a dense theoretical treatment of the emergence of social structure in a small groups laboratory, Couch (1988) offers the following thin description:

> In all groups when a conflict emerged over the assessment to be made of the intergroup negotiations, the representative attempted to make a more favorable assessment than the constituents. . . . In a few instances conflicting assessments were left dangling. . . . In some groups the representatives and constituents became alienated from each other. . . . a few groups became . . . hostile to the opposition. (pp. 22-23)

Couch is describing a complex web of group negotiations and interactions. Conflict, alienation, and hostility are everywhere present, but he does not describe conflict, hostility, or alienation—he simply names them. Social science words do the work of description. Couch glosses what is happening in the groups he is studying.

Medical Work: Glossed Thick Description

In the following example, the researcher glosses a thick description. Strauss (1987) offers an excerpt from an interview with two parents whose young child was born with a congenital heart condition. They had installed a sensitive high-frequency intercom in the baby's room. They had been told by the doctors to watch their baby at all times:

> *We did what we had to do,* . . . *no other choice.* . . . The doctors told us to watch her and *not let her get excited.* . . . They told us to *look for reactions,* so the only way that we could do that was to stay up with her. . . . We were afraid that she would die and we would be asleep. We took turns sleeping and then sitting with her. This lasted for two months. (p. 52)

Strauss then comments on this statement, which was made by the baby's mother. He applies a set of distinctions to the parents' activities. This is his interpretation of their experience:

> *First-order assessment.* Parents do their own assessing, evaluate the situation based on their awareness of the child's condition. Partial, sometimes, half-time, all the time—When does the monitoring take place? How do they know what to monitor? (p. 53)

Here the sociologist interprets a thick description and incorporates the description into a set of theoretical questions that take precedence over the description. He then thinly describes the actual experience. This is glossed thick description.

Typified Thick Description: Response Cries

In the following example, the researcher acts as though he has thick description when in fact he doesn't. Goffman (1981) describes a man walking down the street:

> His general dress and manner have given anyone who views him evidence of his sobriety, innocent intent, suitable aliveness to the situation. . . . His left foot strikes an obtruding piece of pavement and he stumbles. He instantly catches himself, rights himself more or less efficiently, and continues on.
>   Up to this point his competence at walking had been taken for granted. . . . His tripping casts these imputations . . . into doubt. Therefore, before he continues he may well engage in some actions that have nothing to do with laws of mechanics. (pp. 88-89)

These actions, which Goffman calls "response cries," may include the subject's saying things like "What in the world!" (Goffman, 1981, p. 90), "hell," or "shit" (p. 97). But this is not a real man; rather, he is an ideal type that Goffman uses for theoretical purposes. Goffman is not describing anyone's actual experiences, although many readers can likely relate to the experience depicted. A typified, thinly veiled thick description is not actual thick description.

TYPES OF THICK
DESCRIPTION-AS-INSCRIPTION

Social scientists have produced several different types of thick description-as-inscription. There are those who describe micro actions, such as Sudnow playing the piano. Others describe situations of interaction, such as running from a cockfight. Some are historically specific and depict life in an earlier age. Still others describe individuals in particular situations, and some depict social relationships. The descriptions that are offered may be incomplete (to be discussed below), complete, glossed (see above), or intrusive; the researchers' interpretations may intrude into the descriptions. Finally, there are those descriptions in which the authors interpret as they describe—that is, in which interpretation is part of the description (e.g., Sudnow's account of playing the piano in front of his friends). Discussion of each of these types of thick description is necessary. What passes as thick description is often something else.

A Classification of Types

A full or complete thick description is biographical, historical, situational, relational, and interactional. But not every thick description is full or complete. Some thick descriptions focus on relationships, others on individuals, some on situations, and so on. Accordingly, it is possible to classify thick descriptions in terms of the dimensions that are their primary focus. I identify and discuss each of the following types of thick description below: micro, macrohistorical, biographical, situational, relational, interactional, intrusive, incomplete, glossed, purely descriptive, and descriptive and interpretive.

Micro Thick Description

A micro thick description takes a small slice of interaction, experience, or action and records its occurrence in thick detail. Such description often lacks interpretation—it just describes. Here is another example from Sudnow (1978):

> In order to get to the next starting place, I would end it a bit sooner, to give myself time to relocate, feeling the upcoming chord as an encroaching presence whose necessity was fixed by an adherence to the chord chart of the song we were after all "playing together." (p. 31)

Sudnow locates himself within the action he is describing. This is how a micro description is given.

Macrohistorical Thick Description

A macrohistorical description attempts to bring an earlier historical moment or experience alive in vivid detail. Foucault's presentation of the public execution of an attempted assassin illustrates a macrohistorical thick description. The account reveals how micro actions (e.g., the tearing apart of Damiens's body with steel pincers) shape and in fact constitute major historical events.

Biographical Thick Description

A biographically thick description focuses on an individual or a relationship, typically in a situation. In the following excerpt, William Faulkner (1957) describes a key figure in his Snopes family trilogy:

> Will Varner, the present owner of the Old Frenchman place, was the chief man of the county. He was the largest landholder and beat supervisor in one county and Justice of the Peace in the next and election commissioner in both, and hence the fountainhead if not of law at least of advice and suggestion to the countryside. . . . He was a farmer, a usurer, a veterinarian. . . . He was thin as a fence rail and almost as long, with reddish-gray hair and moustaches and little hard bright innocently blue eyes. . . . He was shrewd, secret and merry, of a Rabelaisian turn of mind and very probably still sexually lusty (he had fathered sixteen children to his wife). (p. 5)

Faulkner locates Varner within a social structure (the county), describes what he does, depicts his physical features, and gives him a brief family history. Biographically thick descriptions often connect individuals to situations, as in the next example.

Biographical-Situational Thick Description

> As Gregor Samsa awoke one morning from uneasy dreams he found himself transformed in his hard bed into a gigantic insect. He was lying on his hard, as it were armor-plated, back and when he lifted his head a little he could see his dome-like brown belly divided into stiff arched segments on top of which the bed quilt could hardly keep in position and was about to slide off completely. His numerous legs, which were pitifully thin compared to the rest of his bulk, waved helplessly before his eyes. (Kafka, 1952, p. 19)

This description, a frightening account of the metamorphosis of a human being into an insect, creates a picture of Gregor Samsa for the reader. Kafka succeeds in describing what it would feel like and to awake and see one's body in the shape of an insect.

Biographical-situational thick descriptions re-create the sights, sounds, and feelings of persons and places. They permit entry into the situations of experience. They present these situations and biographies in terms of the points of view of the persons being described.

Situational Thick Description

This excerpt from Jules Henry's (1965) reports on his impressions of life in a nursing home is an example of a thick description of a situation:

> Her room was neat and clean, and the walls were bright yellow. The dresser appeared to be one that ought to belong to the patient, and on it were photographs, toiletries, and a heart-shaped box of candy. The patient's hair was curled and combed and had a ribbon in it. She wore powder, rouge and lipstick. (p. 444)

This description of a situation locates a person in it. It depicts objects in the room and locates them with other objects; the color of the walls and the appearance of the room are included in the description.

The next description, also from Henry's observations, is purely situational:

> The main hall is wider than the two wings and much more attractive. Walls are a pleasing yellow, the ceilings white. . . . the floor is tiled with a grey and black pattern bordered with black. . . . the hall is lined on both sides with chairs and there are divans near the east and west ends. . . . The most comfortable chairs are grouped around a small table. . . . An antique umbrella stand is against one wall, and in an alcove . . . is a religious statue on a marble pedestal. The thumb has been broken off and glued back in place. Birds and flower scenes embroidered on Japanese silk framed in bamboo decorate the walls. (p. 445)

Henry creates a visual picture of a situation with this fine-grained description of the main hall in a nursing home.

Relational Thick Description

A thick relational description brings a relationship alive. Couch's (1988) study, discussed above, examined how triads interact in the laboratory. The following statements describe how intimate and marital partners acted after their lovers or spouses stated that they wanted to end the relationships (all of these statements are quoted in Vaughan, 1986, p. 94):

> She began throwing all my books out the window. Obviously it wasn't the books she was throwing out. (student, age 22, separated after living together 2 years)

He and a friend did a midnight raid on the apartment. He destroyed the furniture and stuff that we had gotten since we'd been together. (floral designer, age 28, separated after living together 4 years)

She slashed the tires on my car. She knew that would get me. She even told me she was going to do it. (salesman, age 30, divorced after 3 years)

He put a knife through my face in our wedding picture. (clinical psychologist, age 36, divorced after 8 years)

These accounts vividly describe actions that symbolize the end of a relationship. The next description locates a relational ending in a situation:

Everybody was home from school. . . . the doorbell rang so the kids answered the door and I was browning the veal and they're saying, "Mom, come to the door. Somebody wants ya." And I said, "But I can't. You tell 'em," you know. They said, "No mom, they said they have to see you." I went to the door and the sheriff handed me a subpoena for a divorce. And the kids are saying, "Mom, what is it?" And they're all standing around me. Here I am with the kids standing around me. "Daddy wants a divorce?" And I started to cry. So, I mean everything is burned and we all sat in here. (quoted in Vaughan, 1986, p. 157)

This thick description re-creates a slice of interactional experience. It contains dialogue and interaction. It takes the reader into the situation and tells how this woman received the information concerning her husband's desire for a divorce. It connects a turning-point experience to its moment of occurrence.

Interactional Thick Description

Interactional thick descriptions, like the example just given, focus on interactions between two or more persons. Here is a man describing how came to beat up his wife:

I come home tired and beat. The house was a mess, the dogs were loose, and she was in the bedroom taking a nap. Supper wasn't even started yet. I fixed a drink, turned on the news. She came out, yelled at me for having that drink. I'd heard it a thousand times before. I couldn't take it anymore. I threw the drink in her face, grabbed her arm and yelled, "Where's my God Damned supper! You never do anything around here." She hit back at me, called me no good. She ran and got my wood carving that I'd been making her for Christmas. She laughed at it, called it stupid and dumb. She threw it

against the wall. That's when I lost it. I ran at her. She called the police.
(quoted in Denzin, 1984b, p. 501)

This statement combines three features of a thick description. It is interactional, situational, and relational. It contains some glosses ("I'd heard it a
thousand times before"; "That's when I lost it"), but it is primarily descriptive. It re-creates, in the man's words, a fight he had with his wife.

Intrusive Thick Description

In an intrusive description, the researcher allows his or her interpretations to enter into and shape the description as he or she reports it. When this
occurs it is difficult to capture the "native's point of view" (Geertz, 1983,
pp. 55-69). The subject's perspective is seen through the researcher's eyes.

Here is an intrusive description. Geertz (1973a) is discussing the moral
and symbolic significance of the cockfight in Bali:

> In the cockfight, man and beast, good and evil, ego and id, the creative
> power of aroused masculinity, and the destructive power of loosened
> animality fuse in a bloody drama of hatred, cruelty, violence, and death.
> (pp. 420-421)

In the next passage, Geertz describes the cockfight:

> Most of the time, in any case, the cocks fly almost immediately at one an-
> other in a wing-beating, head-thrusting, leg-kicking explosion of animal
> fury, so absolute, and in its own way so beautiful, as to be almost abstract, a
> Platonic concept of hate. (p. 422)

In these lines Geertz departs from both pure description and that form of
description that incorporates the native's interpretations into the text (see
below; see also Chapter 7 and Crapanzano, 1986, pp. 68-76).

In the first excerpt above, Geertz attributes all sorts of experiences and
motivations to the Balinese, likening cockfighting to the play between the
Freudian concepts of id and ego and to the aroused forces of destructive
animality (see Crapanzano, 1986, p. 72). In the second excerpt, describing
the cockfight itself, he discusses the actions of the cocks in terms of the Pla-
tonic concept of hate and sees in the fight a beautiful animal fury that is pure
and absolute. These are his interpretations; these are not the words of a Balinese cockfighter. Geertz's interpretations intrude into his descriptions of
the fight. As a result, the reader does not know what a Bali cockfight looks or
feels like. The native's point of view is lost. Geertz asks the reader to see the

fight as he does, but lacking a description of the fight, the reader is left with only Geertz's words.

Incomplete Thick Description

The incomplete thick description begins to present events or experiences in a thick fashion, but at some point interrupts itself and summarizes, or glosses, significant information. In the following excerpt, Isabelle Bertaux-Wiame (1981) quotes from an interview with a young French woman who had left her small village and moved to Paris at the age of 20:

> I was in a bakery—my employers were very nice, but there was only me to deliver the bread to the farms around, with the horse van. It was hard work. And then, one day, it was getting late, it was almost dark, there was a corner in the road, and the horse took fright and bolted. I was that frightened that the very next day, I left the job. I decided to come to Paris to look up an old childhood friend, whose parents had a hotel. I sent word to her and without even waiting for a reply, I set out. (p. 261)

In this statement the young woman explains her going to Paris in terms of the frightening experience she had with the horse van. This is a thick description that is biographical, historical, and interactional. It gives an account for a turning point moment in the woman's life. However, consider the following lines in Bertaux-Wiame's text:

> It was only later on that she [the young woman] mentioned in a whisper that she had had a fiancé but the engagement had been broken off: "I had to go, I had known a young man." (p. 261)

It was not her experience with the horse van that led her to move to Paris, it was her sexual relationship with her fiancé. Bertaux-Wiame offers a dense theoretical interpretation of the "marriage market" in small French villages and its pressures on young women to marry fiancés with whom they have had intimate relations. When her engagement was broken off, the woman was no longer marriageable under the rules of the village; she was not a virgin. If she had stayed in the village, she would have lived the life of a spinster, "letting her 'fault' determine her whole life" (p. 262).

The problem with incomplete thick description is that it glosses the actual experiences that shape what is being described and interpreted. Bertaux-Wiame does not give the reader access to the thoughts and words of this young girl. She lets her own interpretations do the work of actual description. In this respect, an incomplete description is like its intrusive counterpart.

Glossed Thick Description

I have discussed glossed thick description above, in terms of thin descriptions that purport to be thick. The last excerpt from Geertz's description of the cockfight in Bali is an example of glossed thick description.

Purely Descriptive Thick Description

Strictly speaking, there can be no pure description. The words that are used to describe a phenomenon or experience create what is described. I use the word *pure* to reference the relative absence of intrusive interpretations in a description. Here is an example:

> That early morning, in January 1933, only one person was awake on the street . . . call him Samuel Bennet. He wore a trilby had that had been lying by his bedside. . . . In stripped pajamas tight under his arms and torn between the legs, he padded barefoot downstairs and opened the breakfast-room door of his parents' six room house. (Thomas, 1964, p. 3)

This is how Samuel Bennet started his morning. In a few minutes he would destroy family photographs and china as he left his home for good, to make his way as an adult in the outside world. This description offers no intrusive interpretation. Like Sudnow's account of his early days of piano playing, it just describes.

Descriptive and Interpretive Thick Description

Descriptive and interpretive thick description records interpretations that occur within the experience as it is lived. Sudnow's account of how he felt as he played the piano before friends is both descriptive and interpretive. These types of statements are difficult to produce and obtain. They require that a person be able to reflect on experience as it occurs. Such accounts are invaluable, however, because they show how interpretations shape interaction and experience. Here is Sudnow (1978) again:

> From an upright posture I look down at my hands on the piano keyboard during play, with a look that is hardly a look at all. But standing back I find that I proceed through and in a terrain nexus, doing singings with my fingers, so to speak, a single voice at the tips of my fingers, going for each next note in sayings just now and just then. . . . I sing with my fingers, so to speak. (p. 152)

Summary

Table 6.1 provides a summary of the types and forms of thick description described above. The table lists each type and indicates its relative emphasis on the biographical, situational, historical, relational, and interactional dimensions of thick description. The types listed in the table can be divided into three broad categories.[1] Types 1-6 describe the focus of the description: micro, macrohistorical, biographical, situational, relational, interactional. Types 7-9 reflect interpretations of descriptions—that is, whether they are intrusive, incomplete, or glossed. Types 10 and 11 focus solely on description or on a mix of description and interpretation. Types 7-9 are to be avoided. Further examination of the table reveals that some forms are more likely to have an emphasis on one dimension than on another (e.g., biography versus history). A fully triangulated study would contain thick descriptions that encompass each form and content, or focus dimension.

GOOD AND BAD THICK DESCRIPTION

A good thick description as a form of inscription is not glossed, intrusive, or incomplete. A bad description glosses details, inserts the observer's interpretations into the flow of experience that is being recorded, and omits or gives only slight descriptive attention to key details. Above, I have given numerous examples of what I regard as good thick description.

Learning to Listen and Writing Bad Thick Description

In Chapter 7, I will present an interpretation of the following excerpts from my fieldwork on A.A. I offer these here as an example of bad thick description.

In Chapter 5, I argued that the individual who becomes a member of A.A. learns how to listen to what is said in the context of the A.A. world. He or she learns new words as well as new meanings for some words. The member learns to listen. The interpretive researcher must do the same thing. How can the researcher do this? The following example, from field notes that I wrote after I had visited five A.A. meetings, reveals what a researcher should *not* do. I made the following list in my notes under the title "The Structure of an A.A. Meeting."

1. Opening, Welcome.
2. Serenity Prayer—moment of silence.
3. "How It Works" (read by one person, all listen in silence).

Table 6.1

Types of Thick Description

Form	Content and Focus				
	Biographical	*Historical*	*Situational*	*Relational*	*Interactional*
1. Micro description	seldom	possible	yes	yes	yes
2. Macrohistorical description	possible	yes	possible	possible	yes
3. Biographical description	always	yes	yes	possible	yes
4. Situational description	possible	yes	always	possible	possible
5. Relational description	possible	yes	possible	always	yes
6. Interactional description	seldom	possible	yes	yes	always
7. Intrusive description	yes	yes	yes	yes	yes
8. Incomplete description	yes	yes	yes	yes	yes
9. Glossed description	yes	yes	yes	yes	yes
10. Purely descriptive description	yes	yes	yes	yes	yes
11. Descriptive and interpretive description	yes	yes	yes	yes	yes

Note: Yes = content and focus will be present; for forms 7-11 the effect of the focus can be positive or negative. No = content and focus will be absent. Possible = content and focus can be present.

4. The 12 Traditions (read by one person, all listen in silence).

5. Any new members?—Introduced by first name (or newcomers).

6. Announcements—can be made by any member, usually of a new meeting, social announcements, etc.

7. If a new member, the First Step (by tradition with a new member discuss the First Step).

8. In turn each person speaks on the First Step, with the new person given an opportunity to speak, if he or she chooses.

9. If no new member, a topic for discussion is given, may come from the *BIG BOOK*, the thought for the day, any problem dealing with the program—time, the past, responsibility, growing, guilt, tolerance for others.

10. The donation (this is usually made during the readings, but can come anytime in the meeting, depending on the meeting, number of persons present, etc.).

11. The closing—"Does anyone else have anything else they would like to add? If not, we will close in the usual manner." (The Lord's Prayer, all hold hands, speak together, and end with "Keep on Coming Back.")

12. Members depart, break up and leave the table, chat in small gatherings, empty ashtrays, gather up coffee cups, rearrange chairs, etc.

This is flawed thick description. It is intrusive, glossed, and incomplete. My words are all over the place. The voices of A.A. members are nowhere present. I acted "as if" I understood how a meeting worked. I made no mention of biographies, histories, relationships, or interactions. I presented a purely structural picture of a meeting. An inspection of these materials reveals where work needs to be done—that is, precisely on the points just listed. A researcher can put such bad thick description to good use, but only if he or she has the sense to stay in the field long enough to learn what he or she doesn't know. In the next section I take up the problem of the relationship between description and interpretation.

DESCRIPTION, INSCRIPTION,
AND INTERPRETATION

In thick description, the researcher attempts to rescue and secure the meanings, actions, and feelings that are present in an interactional experience (but see Geertz, 1973b, p. 20). Description is necessarily interpretive, as I have shown above. It captures the interpretations that persons bring to the events that have been captured. It records the interpretations that interactants make as the interaction unfolds. It provides the grounds for the researcher's (and the reader's) interpretations of the events and meanings that have been captured. The words that record description are also interpretive.

Thick description involves capturing and representing the meanings a particular action or sequence of actions has for the individuals in question. The capturing of meaningful events is done through the triangulated use of the several methods of recording and capturing life experiences discussed in Chapters 2, 3, and 4 (personal experience stories, self-stories, collecting slices of interaction, interviews). Thick description is biographical and interactional. It connects self-stories and personal histories to specific interactional experiences.

Thick description creates the conditions for thick interpretation, which is the topic of the next chapter. Thick interpretation gives meaning to the descriptions and interpretations given in the events that have been recorded. A good interpretation is one that "takes us to the heart of what is being interpreted" (Geertz, 1973b, p. 18). Thick interpretation attempts to uncover the "conceptual structures that inform our subjects' acts" (Geertz, 1973b, p. 27).

Levels of Meaning

Thick interpretation constructs a system of analysis and understanding that is meaningful within the worlds of lived experience. It assumes that any experience has meaning at two levels: the surface (or the intended) level and the deep (unintended) level (Freud, 1900/1965). Meaning, which must be captured in interpretation, is symbolic. It moves in surface and deep directions at the same time. Thick interpretation attempts to unravel and record these multiple meaning structures that flow from interactional experience. It assumes that multiple meanings will always be present in any situation. No experience ever has the same meaning for two individuals. This is so because meaning is emotional and biographical.

To summarize, thick description has the following characteristics:

1. It builds on multiple, triangulated, biographical methods.
2. It connects biography to lived experience.
3. It is contextual, historical, and interactional.
4. It captures the actual flow of experience of individuals and collectivities in a social situation.
5. It captures the meanings that are present in a sequence of experience.
6. It allows the reader to experience vicariously the essential features of the experiences that are described and are being interpreted.
7. It attempts not to gloss what is being described.

Thick interpretation has the following characteristics (which will be developed in the next chapter):

1. It rests upon and interprets thick descriptions.
2. It assumes that meaning is symbolic and operates at the surface and deep levels.
3. It attempts to unravel the multiple meanings that are present in any interactional experience.
4. It has the objective of constructing an interpretation that is meaningful to the persons studied.

Thick interpretation attempts to conform to the criteria of interpretation discussed in Chapters 3 and 4.

Meanings, Effects, and Interpretations

Recall the discussion of meanings and effects in Chapter 2. Drawing on Ortner (1997a, 1997b), I argued that the effects of a set of practices can be seen in the subjects those practices produce. A focus on effects illuminates the operation of power. Thick description rescues the meanings, experiences, and effects that have occurred in problematic situations. It captures the interpretations that persons bring to the events that have been recorded. It reports those interpretations as they unfold during the interaction. It establishes the grounds for thick interpretation.

CONCLUSION

In this chapter I have offered an extended discussion of thick and thin descriptions and have provided a typology of the various forms of thick description. I have used research illustrations from the actual descriptive work of sociologists, anthropologists, and, in a few cases, writers of fiction (Faulkner and Kafka). These examples indicate that what passes as description is often something else—namely, interpretation. I have provided here some criteria for evaluating descriptions. In the next chapter, I take up the complex problems involved in the interpretation, presentation, and performance of descriptions.

NOTE

1. David R. Maines and Debra J. Rog helped to clarify these divisions for me.

7

Doing Interpretation

This chapter addresses the importance of interpretation and understanding, and describes how interpretation is done. The following topics are addressed: (a) the interpretation of interpretations, (b) what interpretation does and what is interpreted, and (c) types of interpretation. Also, exemplars of thick and thin interpretation are offered, and the relationships among description, interpretation, and understanding are discussed.

In the sense of the term used throughout this volume, *interpretation* is understood to refer to the attempt to explain meaning. An interpreter translates the unfamiliar into the familiar. The act of interpreting gives meaning to experience. *Meaning* refers to that which is in the mind or the thoughts of a person. Meaning, in this sense, involves the signification, purpose, and consequences of a set of experiences for an individual. Meaning is embedded in the stories persons tell about their experiences. Once experiences have been interpreted, their meanings can be understood. In understanding, the meaning of an experience is comprehended and grasped. Understanding can be emotional, cognitive, or both.

Mindful of the meanings of these terms, interpretive interactionists interpret and render understandable turning-point moments of experience, or the epiphanies in the lives of ordinary individuals. They interpret these moments as they have been thickly described. These interpretations make understanding possible. It is not enough just to describe; researchers must produce interpretations and understandings and convey these to their readers.

In Chapter 6, I discussed the various forms of thick description; I will employ the framework developed for analyzing types of thick description in that discussion in this chapter in regard to thick interpretation. I will treat micro, macrohistorical, biographical, situational, relational, interactional, intrusive, incomplete, and glossed interpretations. I will also maintain the distinction, briefly discussed in Chapter 6, between native interpretations and observer interpretations. This will lead to a discussion of the differences between native and social science theories of experience.

THE IMPORTANCE OF
INTERPRETATION AND UNDERSTANDING

I have argued in Chapters 1 and 2 that an interpretive study needs a focus. The project I have chosen examines the existentially problematic, emotional experiences that occur in the lives of ordinary people. These are experiences that make a difference. They connect personal troubles to public issues and to applied programs that address such problems—for example, hot lines for battered women and alcoholism treatment centers for alcoholics. By studying and interpreting these experiences, researchers can hope to comprehend and understand more fully the personal troubles of individuals in the late postmodern period. With such understanding comes knowledge that researchers can share and policy makers can use to help such persons more effectively. Researchers can also use this knowledge in evaluating the programs that have been implemented to assist troubled persons. The designers and implementers of applied programs must grasp, interpret, and understand the perspectives and experiences of those persons they intend to serve if their programs are to be both solid and effective. Ortner (1997b) is clear on this point: Understanding the individual's perspective is "central to the interpretive practice of 'thick description' " (p. 158). Such understanding can help us to see how agency and meaning are culturally constructed through social practices. This argument organizes this chapter.

EXEMPLARS OF INTERPRETATION

Perhaps it will be useful to begin with an example of bad interpretation. Recall my field notes titled "The Structure of an A.A. Meeting," discussed near the end of Chapter 6. In those notes, I described what I believed to be the major moments in an A.A. meeting. Here are the interpretations I wrote:

The A.A. Meeting

Discussion

1. *REFLEXIVITY* builds as each discussant often turns back to what another speaker has said. Seldom are persons explicitly complimented on personal realities that lie behind statements, although points may be praised or built upon.

2. *NAMES*—First names only, unless the group is made up of long-standing persons, when on occasion a first name will be attached to a familiar name—e.g., Bill _____, or Bob _____. Because many persons have the

same first names, elements of personal appearance are added to differentiate speakers, e.g., Ted with the blond hair, etc.

3. *PHRASES*—"You're only human," "You're in the right place," "One day at a time," "First things first," "Easy does it," "I know I can drink again," "The urge has left me," "I pray that it leaves me," "I'm still an alcoholic," "I still have a drink, a binge left in me," "I've come so far," "Being at the tables," "The tables," "The program," "Since I was in treatment," "The club," "I know I'm talking too much," "Does this make sense?" "I used to be a periodic alcoholic."

4. *INTERPRETATION*—Each member/speaker interprets the topic for the evening, or the day, and does so by referring to concrete events in his or her life—"My son-in-law broke his neck at work yesterday. If I were still drinking I wouldn't be able to handle it." Or the reference is more abstract: "How well my life has become since I stopped drinking."

5. From these individual interpretations, strands of meaning and interpretation of the meeting emerge: "This has been a good meeting," "I'm really glad I came tonight," "This has been very good for me," "Thanks for such a good meeting."

6. Out of these interpretations, which are individual, arises an individual's understanding of their place within the program for that particular meeting and evening. They weave strands of interpretation into their understanding of the program and of their own program and reaffirm their bond to the tables and THE PROGRAM. From this reaffirmation flows an understanding that leaves the tables and flows through the person's relational dealings in the everyday world of significant others. They carry these interpretations and meanings—as residue of constructed and reconstructed experience—out into a drinking world, where temptations of drinking and areas of conflict are everywhere.

7. The program works at three levels: (1) admitting and accepting alcoholism; (2) the daily working on the interpersonal problems and character defects that flow from an old personality that drank; (3) daily reminding the person of the rewards of sobriety—how much better things are getting. The meetings and the tables are used to reinforce each of these levels, and as new members come into the program each member can see him- or herself in the despair of the person who has fallen or is still drinking. (field notes, November 2, 1981)

Interpreting a First Interpretation

The notes above reveal several features of the interpretive process. First, they are glosses, or summaries, of experience. They include no knowledge of who the A.A. speakers were. They evidence no understanding of the nuances of A.A. language or A.A. history. They evidence no understanding of the history of this A.A. group. Nor do they indicate how these rituals and the 12 Steps work for the A.A. member. Second, as glosses on experience, they stand as abstractions that record no lived experience. There is no thick description here (see Chapter 6); this is thin description. Third, these notes reveal an arrogance on my part. I assumed that I understood what was going on in an A.A. meeting. In fact, I did not understand what was going on. Fourth, I prejudiced my understandings by focusing only on what occurred at the beginning of the meeting. I thought that what was read was what was most important in the meeting. I would later learn that what is read is important, but not for the reasons that I thought when I took these notes. Fifth, I did not hear what A.A. members said. I assumed that everybody said pretty much the same things. I assumed that I did not have to listen to what each member said. Sixth, I assumed that all A.A. meetings were the same—I later learned that this is not the case.

The interpretations that I offered in my discussion of my notes are also thin and highly speculative. I would later discover that my early understanding of reflexivity in A.A. talk was superficial. A.A. talk is dialogical. It takes as its focus the group and the experiences of the person talking. When an A.A. member talks, he or she speaks to the entire group, not to a specific individual. There is no expectation of any response from individuals to the speaker. The speaker has a self-dialogue with the group.

In a similar manner, I later learned that A.A. members do learn each other's last names and that the tags that I identified, such as "Ted with the blond hair," were the kinds of tags that newcomers use. Within any A.A. meeting, one or more members will know the biography that stands behind a first name, including (often) the person's last name. The phrases that I recorded ("One day at a time" and so on) are part of A.A. talk in any A.A. meeting. They reflect how the speakers have located themselves within A.A. folklore and have appropriated that folklore for their self-stories. I would later learn that one can identify members' length of membership by the segment of A.A. folklore they characteristically use when they talk. I did not know this when I wrote these notes and interpretations.

My interpretations of the talk I had heard at meetings failed to grasp how a member weaves talking into his or her personal life. I failed to see that an essential part of A.A. talk is being able to locate an experience in one's life that could be a reason for drinking and then showing how one in fact did not drink. I failed to grasp the single-minded goal of the A.A. member, which is to stay sober at any cost. My statements under point 7 above hinted at this understanding, but failed to grasp its significance for the A.A. member. These notes reveal how a researcher who does not know how to listen takes field notes and makes interpretations.

Taking Time

Interpretation is a temporal process. First, it takes time for a researcher to learn the language of the group he or she is studying. Second, as I have argued in Chapter 6, the researcher must learn the biographies of the persons who speak the language. This knowledge takes the researcher further into the social structure of the group being studied. It shows how each individual's life experiences shape how he or she talks, uses the language, and tells stories. Third, the researcher must learn the relationships that exist among the persons in the group. Fourth, the interpreter must be able to call up in him- or herself the range of meanings that any word or phrase has for a group member. This process of taking the attitude of the other (Mead, 1934) is a linguistic and emotional one. The researcher can hope to achieve this only after he or she has become immersed in the group. The researcher, to repeat a point made earlier, must be able to live him- or herself into the life experiences of the group. If the researcher does not do so, he or she will write only superficial, thin interpretations.

It was 3 years before I felt completely comfortable with the A.A. language and the meaning structures that lie behind that language. Because interpretation is a temporal process, researchers are wise to study those areas of social life in which they already have some intimate familiarity. By doing so, they can draw upon the stocks of knowledge that they have built up out of previous life experiences. This is one of the consequences of C. Wright Mills's directive to connect personal biography with sociological inquiry.

WHAT INTERPRETATION DOES

As I have noted, interpretation builds on description. It gives meaning to experiences that have been thickly described. Interpretation makes sense out of expressions of experience. The experience that is made sense of is expressed symbolically (see below). These symbolic expressions often take the form of personal experience stories and self-stories. In some instances, meaningful experience may be expressed dramatically, in the form of performed texts or other kinds of performances (Bruner, 1986, p. 7; Turner, 1986a). Interpretive interactionists interpret and perform symbolic and interactional expressions of meaningful, turning-point experiences.

Types of Interpreters

Interpretation is done by interpreters, of which there are two types: (a) the people who have actually experienced what is described and (b) so-called well-informed experts, who are often ethnographers, sociologists, or anthropologists. The two different types of interpreters (local and social science) often give different meanings to the same set of thickly described experiences. (I discuss the differences in these two types of interpretations below.)

Interpretation clarifies and untangles the meanings that are produced by a set of experiences. It does so within an interpretive framework that is meaningful to those who have experienced the event in question—that is, interpretation utilizes experience-near concepts and interpretations. Interpretation, as Geertz (1973b, p. 27) argues, illuminates the meanings and conceptual structures that organize a subject's experience.

Theories of Interpretation

What does this mean? It means that individuals have working theories of their own conduct and their own experiences. These theories derive from the concepts the individuals share with their fellows. They are contained in the oral and printed cultural texts of the group. These theories are based on the "local knowledge" (Geertz, 1983) that individuals and groups have about those experiences that matter to them. These theories are pragmatic— that is, they work (see James, 1955; Peirce, 1934). They work because they give meaning to problematic experiences. These meanings allow persons to deal with the problems that confront them. These theories may be fatalistic, idealistic, religious, spiritual, ideological, political, or fantastic. They may draw from social science theories or they may be passed from one generation to the next, whether through oral or written tradition.

Here is an example of a local theory of interpretation. The speaker has been in A.A. and sober for 10 years.

> I used to drink everyday. Then I came to A.A. and learned that I got a disease called alcoholism. I got sober by coming to meetings, reading the Big Book, working the Steps and getting myself a sponsor. I got a spiritual program and I work with newcomers. I haven't had a drink since I started doing all of these things. (male, 45 years old, divorced, house painter)

Narratives, Stories, and Local Theories of Interpretation

The statement above contains the speaker's interpretation of why he is sober. It invokes A.A.'s theory of alcoholism (a disease) and recovery (go to meetings, read the Big Book, work with others, and so on). The theory says that if you do these things, you will get sober and stay sober. He did these things, and he has been sober for 10 years. He is pragmatically using A.A.'s theory to help him deal with a problem in his life. His theory is A.A.'s theory. In the above account he has given a glossed statement of this theory. (I will discuss glossed interpretations in detail below.) His statement takes the form of an abbreviated narrative, or story. It has a beginning, a middle, and an end. He states that he used to drink every day, and then he started coming to A.A. meetings, where he learned that he has a disease called alcoholism. In A.A. (the middle part of his narrative), he acquired a spiritual program. The end of his story states that he hasn't had a drink since he started doing all of these things.

A major goal of the researcher in conducting interpretation is to uncover the theories, often revealed through stories, that structure the experiences of the persons being studied. Interpretive interactionism assumes, as I have argued in Chapters 1 and 2, that for certain purposes all the researcher needs to do is uncover these local theories of interpretation. When the researcher has done so, he or she will have uncovered the conceptual structures that inform the subject's actions. Unless the researcher accomplishes this, he or she will be ignoring the subject's point of view. Without this point of view, the researcher is likely to build his or her evaluations or interpretations of the subject's actions on theories that are not in tune with the subject's actual experiences. When this occurs, applied research programs risk failure. They will not be in touch with the people they are intended to serve. There will be occasions, however, when a subject's theory is incomplete, biased, and self-serving. When this occurs, the researcher must go beyond the subject's definitions of experience to other interpretations (see the discussion below).

The seeds of interpretation, then, are always contained within the experiences that have been thickly described. But the researcher must collect and locate these experiences within the group and its cultural meanings. The interpreter needs to learn how to see and hear these theories. This is what interpretation does.

Interpretation Is Symbolic

In Chapter 6, I suggested that experience always has at least two levels of meaning: the surface and the deep. What an act means on the surface is perhaps not always what it means at a deeper, more symbolic level. An event, because it is experienced and captured within language, is symbolic. This means that interpretation is always symbolic. First, an event or experience can be interpreted in multiple ways. For example, a simple "Hello," spoken abruptly, in anger, does not carry the same meaning as "Hello" spoken with a smile and accompanied by a warm handshake. If interpretation is symbolic, then the researcher must grasp and understand the multiple meanings that are conveyed by words, phrases, and gestures. This means that interpretation must always be contextualized. Words have different meanings in different contexts.

Interpretation is symbolic in a second way as well. The expressions of the meanings of an experience are given in symbolically meaningful ways, often as stories, or narratives. These symbolic expressions may extend beyond storytelling practices to rituals and ritual performances, social dramas, and statements given in the cultural texts of the group (see Bruner, 1986; Turner, 1986b, p. 41). The researcher must collect and study these symbolic expressions of meaningful experience (see Rosaldo, 1986). Through studying them, the researcher can learn how subjects collectively and individually define themselves in their moments of crisis.

TYPES OF
INTERPRETATION AND EXEMPLARS

An observer may write or secure several different types of interpretations. As I noted at the beginning of this chapter, interpretations, like the descriptions they build upon, may be micro, macrohistorical, biographical, situational, relational, interactional, intrusive, incomplete, glossed, and thick or thin. Rather than repeat the discussion of some of these types offered in Chapter 6 in relation to thick description, I focus here on only the following types of interpretation: thin, thick, native, observer, analytic, descriptive-contextual, and relational-interactional.

Thin Interpretation: Response Cries

A thin interpretation is a gloss. It often offers a causal interpretation of a sequence of action—for example, "Person A ran across the road because the bus was coming." Thin interpretation, like its counterpart, thin description, does not give detail on context, biography, interaction, history, or social relationships. Here is an example. Recall the discussion in Chapter 6 of Goffman's (1981) man who stumbles while walking along the street. When this man falters, he utters an apology, or account, to others who may have seen him stumble. He engages, Goffman asserts, in the following action: "Our subject externalizes a presumed inward state and acts so as to make discernible the special circumstances which presumably produced it. He tells a little story in the situation" (p. 89). In so doing, Goffman argues, this man breaks the prescriptive rule of communication of "no talking to oneself in public" (p. 88). This is a thin, glossed, analytic interpretation (see below). It lacks context, biography, history, and interaction. It does not rest on thick description.

Thick Interpretation: Alcoholic Slips

Thick interpretation elaborates and builds upon thick description (see the discussion at the end of Chapter 6). Thick interpretation incorporates context, interaction, and history. Consider the following, which is taken from my book *The Recovering Alcoholic* (Denzin, 1987b). I am discussing the slips, or relapses, of alcoholics after they have attended A.A. for a period of time:

> Alcoholics who slip do so only to the extent that they define themselves as "situational alcoholics." Such members come to A.A. out of an attempt to solve a particular problem in their life. When that problem is solved they relinquish the identity of alcoholic and return to previous conceptions of themselves. (p. 151)

When the process described here occurs, if the member confronts a problem that used to result in his or her drinking, a relapse will occur. The above statement interprets slips in light of context, history, biography, and interaction. It is based on an extensive description of alcoholic identities (Denzin, 1987b, chap. 5).

Native Interpretation, Contextual-Relational: Battered Wives

A native interpretation, as discussed above, states the meaning of an experience in terms of the local knowledge of the individuals actually involved in the experience. A native interpretation may be thick or thin. Here is an example. Johnson and Ferraro (1984) quote the following statement from a woman who has been beaten by her alcoholic husband. She explains her decision to leave him after he made a direct threat on her life. Her explanation takes the form of a story:

> It was like a pendulum. He'd swing to the extremes both ways. He'd get drunk and beat me up, and then he'd get sober and treat me like a queen. One day he put a gun to my head and pulled the trigger. It wasn't loaded. But that's when I decided I'd had it. I sued for separation of property. (p. 121)

This statement contains an interpretation of the woman's actions. She made the decision to leave when her husband put a gun to her head. This interpretation is contextual, relational, historical, and interactional.

Observer Interpretation

Johnson and Ferraro (1984) state, in regard to the above case and others like it, that "women who suddenly realize that their lives are literally in danger may begin the victimization process. . . . Life itself is more important to maintain than the relationship" (p. 121). This interpretation grows out of this woman's interpretation of her experiences. It makes sense in light of her statement. It is unlike my earlier interpretation of the A.A. meeting or Geertz's reading of the Balinese cockfight (see below). Each of these other interpretations imposes the observer's framework on the native's experiences.

Types of Observer Interpretations: Voices and Dialogue

An observer interpretation may also be thick or thin. It may build upon local interpretations or it may impose the observer's own interpretation on the experiences that have been described. An observer interpretation may be *monologic,* suppressing the voices of those studied. Such an interpretation presents the subjects' experiences through the observer's words (see the examples from Geertz). On the other hand, observer interpretations may be *dialogic* and *polyphonic;* that is, they may reflect a dialogue between the observer and those studied, and may allow many different voices and interpretations to speak from the writer's text (see Bakhtin, 1981; Bruner, 1986; see also the examples below). Dialogic and polyphonic interpretations are preferable, because they allow multiple voices to be heard.

Dialogic and Polyphonic Interpretation: 12 Stepping

Here is an example of a dialogic, polyphonic interpretation. It also is taken from my study of the recovering alcoholic. In the following excerpt, four A.A. members are discussing what "12 Stepping" means to them. (In A.A., *12 Stepping* refers to carrying the A.A. message to a suffering alcoholic.)

Tn: I have a problem. I got a neighbor who is fighting with this thing [alcoholism]. Yesterday I went over and I gave it to him straight. I said . . . he needed help.

Ws: I'm Ws. I'm an alcoholic. I wasn't going to speak today. Eight years ago today they took me to the fifth floor . . . for crazies. I was Twelve Stepped while I was there. You had a successful Twelve Step. . . . You came back sober. . . .

Khy: I'm Khy. I'm an alcoholic. I don't know what got me sober. It was many different things. It had to be a sum that was greater than its parts. . . .

Dv: I'm Dv. I'm an alcoholic. . . . I'm working with someone right now. He's sober . . . then drunk . . . then sober, then drunk. I don't know how it works. I know I was successfully Twelve Stepped. (Denzin, 1987b, p. 111)

In this excerpt, four voices speak. Each speaker defines in his or her own words the meaning of 12 Stepping. Tn speaks about carrying the message to his neighbor. Ws describes his own experiences while he was on a psychiatric ward. Khy describes her recovery, and Dv discusses how he is working with an alcoholic who is still drinking. I call this is a dialogic, polyphonic, or multivoiced interpretation.

Analytic Interpretation

Analytic interpretation imposes an abstract, often causal scheme on a set of events or experiences. It typically derives from a theory the observer has imported into the research situation, although it may be derived from the setting (see Geertz's propositions about the Balinese cockfight and discussion below).

Descriptive-Contextual Interpretation: Making Jazz

Descriptive-contextual interpretation is fitted to the concrete experiences being interpreted. It is necessarily biographical and historical, idiographic, and emic. It is particularizing and interprets a case or experience in terms of its unique properties and dimensions. A descriptive-contextual interpretation should be multivoiced (polyphonic) and dialogical, although this may not always be possible or even necessary. Here is David Sudnow (1978) talking about his advancing ability to make jazz music on the piano:

As the time got into the fingers, hands, arms, shoulders, everywhere, altogether new relationships between chords and paths were being fulfilled. . . . I would do jazz sayings that increasingly brought my full "vocabular" resources, my full range of wayful reaching, into the service of the jazz on the records. (p. 141)

In this statement Sudnow interprets his ability to make music like the music on the records. He does this in terms of time: time getting into his fingers, hands, arms, and shoulders. This is a thick, descriptive, contextual, interactional interpretation.

Factual and Interpretive Descriptive Interpretation

There are two types of descriptive interpretation: factual and interpretive. A descriptive-contextual interpretation may presume to record a set of experiences objectively, or factually. The interpretive descriptive interpretation rests on native narrative accounts of experiences. An objective-descriptive interpretation attempts to work with facts. An interpretive narrative account presents experiences as they have been interpreted and makes no pretense about being factually accurate or any claims about resting on facts per se (see the discussion below and the discussion of 12 Stepping above).

Relational-Interactional Interpretation

Relational-interactional interpretation makes sense of a set of experiences in terms of the social relationships and interactions that occur in the situation. *All* interpretations should be relational and interactional, as well as contextual. Such interpretations should rest on thick descriptions and should be nonanalytic.

There are a number of interrelationships among the types of interpretation described above. I turn now to extended discussion of some of these.

Thin, Analytic, Observer-Based Interpretation

Geertz and the Balinese Cockfight

In Chapter 6, I offered several excerpts from Geertz's study of the cockfight in Bali and suggested that his descriptions too often blur interpretations with descriptions. Here is another statement by Geertz (1973a):

> Enacted and re-enacted, so far without end, the cockfight enables the Balinese, as read and reread, Macbeth enables us, to see a dimension of his own subjectivity. . . . In the cockfight, then, the Balinese forms and discovers his temperament and his society's temper at the same time. (pp. 450-451)

What does this statement mean? Geertz is comparing the text of the cockfight to a Shakespearean play and is suggesting that both texts create subjective understandings for their readers. How does he know this? These are Geertz's interpretations of the cockfight. They are not the meanings that a Balinese male or female brings to the occasion of a cockfight.

Consider the following, more abstract interpretation of the cockfight. Here Geertz (1973a) states his understandings in terms of propositions:

1. The closer the identification of cock and man . . . the more the man will advance his best . . . cock.
2. The greater the emotion that will be involved and the more the general absorption in the match . . . the "solider" the citizens who will be gaming. (p. 441)

Geertz states that this is a formal paradigm, designed to display the logical, "not the causal structure of cockfighting" (p. 441). In these two propositions he offers what I call an analytic interpretation (see above and the discussion below) of a key cultural text. It contains several problematic descriptions: "identification," "best cock," "greater the emotion," "general absorption," "solid citizens." Geertz does not supply the meanings of these terms. These terms and the interpretations that Geertz builds with them stand several levels above the actual experience of the cockfight.

Geertz's interpretations are decontextual, nonrelational, and noninteractional. They are thinly disguised as thick interpretations. They are monologic and suppress the natives' voices. They are not dialogical, for Geertz imposes his interpretations on the natives' experiences. They presume a factually accurate rendering of the form and content of the cockfight (e.g., the propositions), but missing are the local account and interpretation of the cockfight. This means we have only Geertz's theory of the cockfight. There is no way of knowing if his theory fits the interpretations held by the participants in this event.

Lindesmith, the Negative Case, and Analytic Interpretation

Further elaboration of analytic interpretation is required. I draw here on the work of Alfred Lindesmith (1947, 1952), whose work on the logic of analytic induction closely parallels what I am terming *analytic interpretation*. Analytic induction (and interpretation) is the process of progressively defining and interpreting the phenomenon to be understood. Described abstractly, it involves the following steps:

1. Formulating a definition of the phenomenon
2. Formulating an initial interpretation of the phenomenon
3. Inspecting a case, or series of cases, in light of this interpretation
4. Reformulating the interpretation as negative cases, or empirical irregularities, emerge

5. Continuing this process until a universal or all-encompassing interpretation of every case has been formulated (see Denzin, 1978, p. 192; 1989b, chap. 8)

Lindesmith (1952, p. 492) has termed this process *analytic induction.* I call it analytic interpretation because the inductive process (working from facts to regularities) is always interpretive (see Athens, 1984a, 1984b). Lindesmith explains:

> The principle that governs the selection of cases to test a theory is that the chances of discovering a decisive negative case should be maximized. The investigator who has a working hypothesis concerning his data becomes aware of certain areas of critical importance. . . . He knows that its weaknesses will be more clearly and quickly exposed if he proceeds to the investigation of these critical cases. This involves going out of one's way to look for negating evidence. (p. 492)

Here is an example from Lindesmith's (1947) research on opiate addiction. Lindesmith was attempting to formulate a sociological theory of drug addiction. He began with the hypothesis that persons who do not know that a drug they are taking is addictive cannot become addicted. He also hypothesized that persons will become addicted if they know they are taking an addictive drug and if they have taken such a drug long enough to experience distress or withdrawal when the drug is not available. This hypothesis was destroyed when Lindesmith interviewed a physician who had taken morphine for several weeks, knew of the drug's addictive qualities, and did not become addicted. This negative case led Lindesmith to reformulate his hypotheses. He next posited that persons become addicts when they recognize and perceive the significance of withdrawal distress and then take the drug to remove the effects of withdrawal (see also Becker, 2001, p. 258).

Lindesmith (1947) comments on his search for and use of negative cases:

> Each succeeding tentative formulation . . . was based on that which had preceded it. The eventual hypothesis altered the preceding formulations sufficiently to include the cases which earlier had appeared as exceptions to the theory postulated. (pp. 9-10)

Lindesmith goes on to discuss how he explicitly sought out negative cases, both in his interviews with addicts and in the research literature. He argues that none of those cases contradicted his final hypothesis.

The researcher's intent in using analytic interpretation is to formulate interpretations that apply to every instance of the phenomenon examined.

These interpretations must fit into a meaningful, interpretive whole, so that no case is excluded.

Problems and Advantages of Analytic Interpretation

The use of analytic interpretation involves four basic problems. First, analytic interpretation rests on a model of science that assumes the formulation of hypotheses and the testing of theories. Second, it assumes that facts can be gathered and that these facts will offer tests of a theory. In this sense, the analytic approach often fails to deal with the socially constructed nature of facts (Fielding & Fielding, 1986, p. 33). "Objective truth" can never be found, and purely objective, noninterpretive tests of a theory can never be made (see Lincoln & Guba, 1985, p. 283). Third, analytic interpretation reduces the interpretive process to a set of decontextualized, nonbiographical propositions. As a result, individual, lived experiences disappear from the writer's text. Interpretive interactionism, as I have noted in Chapter 2, rejects hypothesis and theory testing. Fourth, analytic interpretation, as noted above, suppresses the voices of the natives. This leads to the production of monologic texts that displace the interpretations of natives.

There are, however, advantages to the use of analytic interpretation, and these are balanced against the negative features just discussed. First, as an interpretive strategy, analytic interpretation forces the researcher to specify clearly the phenomenon and the research question under investigation. Second, it alerts the researcher to unique or negative cases that he or she might otherwise ignore. Third, it forces the researcher to judge his or her interpretations constantly against lived experiences. Analytic interpretation is to be avoided if it leads the researcher to write interpretations that are not dialogic, thick, and multivoiced.

Thick, Contextual, Interactional, Multivoiced Interpretation

Ilongot Hunting Stories

Rosaldo's (1986) study of the hunting stories that Ilongot men tell one another provides an illustration of a thick, multivoiced, contextual interpretation. The Ilongots number about 3,500. They live in the uplands northeast of Manila in the Philippines. They are headhunters, although they subsist by hunting deer and wild pig and by cultivating gardens. Their stories relate, with high drama, hunts, the killing of wild animals, risk taking, fears of death, and the final victory of man over animal. Rosaldo presents and analyzes several of these stories. Here is a portion of one of them:

> Let's go to a far place . . . and we'll hunt there. And after we've eaten game
> we'll go to the fork of the Mabu since it's there we can really hunt. . . .
> We're going to hunt the highest mountains. (p. 104)

In another story, a monster is addressing the headhunters' wives:

> Don't go and get their vaginas. . . . And their penises, Uh, they'll make us
> drunk. That's when, they say, friend, they chopped away, these Ilongots
> did, the ones raided, got lost, and came upon them. Now by stealth there
> they chopped them up. (p. 124)

Rosaldo offers the following interpretation of these stories:

> The stories these Ilongot men tell about themselves both reflect what actu-
> ally happened and define the kinds of experiences they seek out on future
> hunts. Indeed, their very postures while hunting resemble those used in
> storytelling, and in this respect the story informs the experience of hunt-
> ing. . . . Ilongot huntsmen experience themselves as the main characters in
> their own stories. (p. 134)

Rosaldo's reading of these stories fits them to the actual and imagined experiences of the hunters. He shows how their stories structure future hunts. In
this sense, he joins a native theory of interpretation with his own interpretation of the stories. Note that he does not inquire into the "factual" accuracy
of the stories. He treats them as accounts of events that may or may not have
happened. In this sense, he reads the stories as symbolic expressions of the
lived experiences of the Ilongot hunters.

Battered Wives as Victims

Johnson and Ferraro (1984) discuss the victimized self, which they define as "a complex mixture of feelings and thoughts based on the individual's overriding feeling of having been violated, exploited, or wronged by
another person or persons" (p. 119). Based on their extensive analysis of the
experiences of battered wives, they observe:

> The victimized self emerges during moments of existential threat, and it
> dissolves when one takes actions to construct new, safer living condi-
> tions. . . . [It] emerges when the rationalizations of violence and abuse be-
> gin to lose their power. (p. 121)

Johnson and Ferraro then contextualize this interpretation, making it biographical and interactional through an interpretive reading of the stories battered wives tell about their marriages. Their final interpretive theory is multivoiced and dialogical. It builds on native interpretations and in fact simply articulates what is implicit in those interpretations. This is what thick interpretation is supposed to do: It brings to life and illuminates interpretive theories that already exist in the worlds of lived experience.

I turn now to a discussion of performances and the use of various creative analytic practices (Richardson, 2000) to represent interpretation.

PERFORMING AND
REPRESENTING INTERPRETATION

The *performed text* interacts with a prior text, whether field notes, interviews, or a literary work (see Denzin, 1997, pp. 98-99). This interaction produces the performance, the interpretive event. The meaning of an interpretation is thus given in the performance. Multiple meanings and pleasures can be brought to the performance site, including those that are aesthetic, intellectual, emotional, participatory, political, and commemorative of various forms of cultural memory. The performance text reports upon (brings news from), dramatizes, and critiques some segment of ongoing cultural life.

Performance texts can take several different forms, including dramatic texts, such as rituals, poems, and plays meant to be performed; natural texts, or transcriptions of everyday conversations turned into natural performances; field notes and interviews turned into performances; and improvisational, critical ethnodramas that merge natural-script dialogues with dramatized scenes and the use of composite characters (see Mienczakowski, 1995).

These dramatic forms are to be distinguished from "staged readings," in which one or more persons hold scripts of the text and read from it. Staged readings are text-centered productions and may involve rehearsals by readers-as-performers. Improvised staged readings call for the stage director (the author of the paper) to hand out parts of the script to members of the audience, who then read on cue. Performance texts attempt to move away from the written texts from which they come, although some may preserve the content of those texts onstage even as they involve audience members as coperformers.

Below, I discuss briefly three performance-representational forms: poetry, short stories, and layered texts.

Poetry

Interpretations may be represented and performed in poetic form. In the following lines, a field-worker describes her relationship to those she is studying:

> We are tourists . . .
> strayed from Cancun and Chichen Itza
> and the great Mayan past.
> In the name of education
> we are voyeurs in your struggle,
> trespassers in your reality.
> Powerless, Helpless, Useless, Dangerous,
> "Do not think badly of us."

(Simonelli, 2000, pp. 105-106)

Short Stories

Jean Halley (2000) begins her first-person short story about a childhood trauma thus:

> This is my history, my remembering. That is all. I guess I am choosing to remember, both to leave my history and to return. I am only too aware that it will always be with me. (p. 349)

And this is what will always be with her, a memory of sitting on her grandfather's lap as a young girl:

> Let me tell you a memory. . . . It is a memory of shame. I am sitting on Mac's lap. . . . Mac has his hand in my shirt, and he is touching my absolutely flat child chest. I can tell you now I did not like this. . . . In the memory, Gram walks in . . . and she sees what is happening. There are so many things I would like to be able to tell you now. . . . But, it is too late . . . for lying. So I will tell you what Gram did. She walked in and saw what was happening. And then, she turned around and walked out. (p. 358)

Layered Texts

In a layered text, performance writing is interspersed with interpretation. Carol Rambo Ronai (1998, 1999) has helped to create this writing form. She writes:

Barefoot, wearing a push-up bra and t-back strap, the screams from the men deafen me. . . . A drunk bellows, "fifteen bucks." . . . I scan the room and smile back at the crowd, numb with alcohol, trying to get a fix on the situation. I should feel something—fear-shame, disgust, dismay—something. Yet I am suspended in an odyssey of lights. . . . As I exit the stage, Kitty, the troupe manager, says, "That went well." . . .
Drawing on field notes from the evening's events, this is a "layered account" about performing with Kitty's troupe. From these materials, I wish to draw a picture of what it was like to be an ethnographer/dancer/wrestler that night, emphasizing the ambiguity and the loose coupling of the performer's identities with their social situations. . . . I have used Derrida's discussion of mystic sketch pad to show how impressions from the world become . . . layered on the existing stocks of knowledge. . . . Lived experience can also be described as a layering process. (Ronai, 1999, pp. 114-115)

Elsewhere, Ronai (1998) says, "The layered account, a postmodern writing format . . . is used as a vehicle to decenter the authority of the 'scientific' voice" (p. 407). Thus the form moves back and forth between inscriptions of experience and interpretive reflections on those representations.

I turn now to a discussion of understanding and its relationship to interpretation.

UNDERSTANDING

Interpretation is the clarification of meaning. Understanding is the process of interpreting, knowing, and comprehending the meaning that is felt, intended, and expressed by another (Denzin, 1984a, pp. 282-284). Interpretation precedes understanding. It has its meaning in the description of an individual's actions within a framework that is meaningful to that person. Interpretation dissects units of experience into relevant segments (statements, sequences, actions) that have meaning.

Just as description provides the framework for interpretation, so too does interpretation create the conditions for understanding. Understanding and interpretation, Schwandt (1999, p. 455) notes, are practical moral activities that involve dialogue. Understanding is an interactional process. It is relational and dialogical. It involves a process in which an individual learns his or her way into conversation with another. During this process, misunderstandings can take place (Schwandt, 1999, p. 455).

Understanding requires that one person enter into the life of another and experience for him- or herself the same or similar experiences as the other (Denzin, 1984a, p. 137). The subjective interpretation of another's emotional experience from one's own standpoint is central to emotional understanding

(Denzin, 1984a, p. 137). This means that shared and shareable emotionality lies at the center of the process of understanding. Two elements are basic to understanding: interpretation and shared experience. A brief discussion of each is necessary.

Interpretation. A researcher cannot understand the experiences of another person until he or she has interpreted them. This means that the conditions of thick description must be present before meaningful interpretation can occur. For example, a violent act has no meaning out of context. In order to interpret such a symbolic act, the reader must know what came before the violence. The reader must also know what followed that action. Once the context is established, the meaning of the act emerges. This is how description and interpretation work together.

Shared experience. Understanding, as suggested above, requires that the researcher be able to enter into, or take the point of view of, another's experience. Mead (1934) calls this "taking the attitude of the other." Various other terms have been used to describe this process, including *sympathy, empathy, imagination, Verstehen,* and *sympathetic understanding* (see Denzin, 1984a, p. 133). Whatever term is used, the meaning is essentially the same: The researcher must be able to project him- or herself into the experiences of the other. This means that the experiences of the other must call up in the researcher feelings similar to those that the other has experienced. The individual who seeks to understand must be able to see the experiences of the other from that person's point of view. This is what I mean when I refer to researchers' living their way into and through the lives of others. The researcher must share, if only indirectly, in the emotional experiences of the other. If the researcher cannot do this, he or she is sure to produce only shallow, empty, spurious, and one-sided interpretation and understanding.

Types of Understanding

There are two basic forms of understanding: cognitive and emotional (Denzin, 1984a, pp. 145-156). Emotional understanding moves along emotional lines, as emotionality, self-feelings, and shared experience enter into the interactional-interpretive process. Cognitive understanding, in contrast, is rational, orderly, logical, and detached from emotional feeling. Emotional understanding embraces emotion and displaces logic, reason, and rationality. In practice it is difficult, if not impossible, to separate these two forms of understanding, because emotions and cognitions blur together in individuals' streams of experience (James, 1890/1950, pp. 185-187).

Understanding may also be dissected into two additional categories. The first of these is *spurious understanding,* which occurs when an individual only superficially enters into the experiences of another. In spurious understanding, a person projects his or her own understandings onto another, often because the person is unwilling to enter into the other's point of view or because the person mistakes his or her own feelings for the feelings of the other. Spurious understanding may also be produced by a person's thin or inattentive descriptions of the actions and experiences of another.

The second category of understanding that I wish to introduce is *true* or *authentic emotional understanding.* This occurs when one person enters into the experiences of another and reproduces or experiences feelings similar to those felt by the other. This means that shared emotional experience underlies authentic emotional understanding.

Given the distinctions described above, it is now possible to introduce one additional clarification. Corresponding to cognitive and emotional understandings are cognitive and emotional interpretations. Cognitive interpretations strip emotion from experience. They deal with the bare facts. They are based on thin descriptions. Emotional interpretations overflow with emotion and feeling.

An Illustration

Consider the following statement made by a recovering alcoholic who has slipped after 6 years of continuous sobriety. He is speaking to another A.A. member; the two are in a detox center.

> When I'm sober it doesn't bother me—that thing that happened 8 years ago [he molested a child]. When I drink it's right in front of me and I want to do it again. I go crazy thinking about it. Maybe that's why I started drinking again so I could think these insane, crazy thoughts. I don't know. Look where the drinking has got me now. A.'s [his ex-wife] got me over a barrel. She's got the house, the car, the money. Everything. What can I do? I can stay sober for a few weeks, then it all comes back to me. And then I drink. What can I do? Hell, she made me so damned mad I hit her and threw her up against the wall. Now I can't go home.
>
> I know I'm an alcoholic. I know the program. I know how to stay sober but I can't. You know I stopped coming to meetings. I know I can't stop drinking after one drink. I even accept that I'm an alcoholic. I don't feel it in my gut, though. I still think I can drink and control the stuff. I still want

to drink. I can say the words "I'm an alcoholic," but I don't feel them. Hell, am I just crazy? (from a field conversation, as reported, August 1, 1985)

All of the forms of understanding and interpretation discussed above are present in this self-story. The speaker has a cognitive understanding and interpretation of his alcoholism. He emotionally understands the pain that he creates for himself when he drinks. But he does not feel deep inside himself that he is an alcoholic. He does not have an emotional understanding and interpretation of his situation. His understanding is superficial, or spurious. He dissociates himself from the negative experiences he creates when he drinks. He does not have a true or authentic grasp and understanding of what his alcoholism is doing and has done to him. In a parallel manner, he cognitively grasps A.A.'s program, but he has failed to live that program into his life. He knows this, but he hasn't connected this cognitive knowledge to deep, emotional, self-understandings.

These forms of understanding and interpretation structure and organize the meanings and understandings that persons form about themselves and others. They are present, in some form, in most if not all interactions a person moves through on a daily basis. Because they are woven into the fabric of everyday life, they must become part of the interpretive sociologist's vocabulary. But more than just this is involved. These forms and modes of understanding and interpretation define the essential goals of interpretation. Stated succinctly, the goal of interpretation is *to build true, authentic understandings of the phenomenon under investigation.* This is why thick description is so critical to interpretive studies. It creates verisimilitude, thereby allowing the reader to enter into the emotional experiences of the persons being studied.

Understanding and Applied Research

In the preceding chapters I have argued that much applied, evaluative research assumes the formulation and existence of interpretations and understandings of the problems being addressed by a specific program. I have also argued for a consideration of the perspectives (local theories) of those persons served by a program. Evaluators form cognitive and emotional understandings that may be spurious, and they build interpretations that are often based on skewed or biased pictures of the phenomena in question. Applied, evaluative research needs a theory of interpretation and understanding that is grounded in the distinctions made above.

Grief and a Headhunter's Rage

Let's return to Rosaldo and the Ilongot hunters, who are, as noted earlier, headhunters. When Rosaldo (1984) asked the men why they engaged in head-hunting, he was invariably told that "the rage in bereavement could impell men to headhunt" (p. 179). He always dismissed this answer as being too simplistic, thin, and implausible. However, in 1981 his wife, Michelle Rosaldo, fell to her death in the Philippines. The Rosaldos were doing research on the Ilongot at the time. He describes his experiences after this event:

> I sobbed, but rage blocked the tears. . . . I felt in my chest the deep cutting pain of sorrow almost beyond endurance, the cadaverous cold of realizing the finality of death, the trembling beginning in my abdomen and spreading through my body as a form of wailing. . . . Writing in my journal six weeks after Shelly's death, I noted: "If I ever return to anthropology by writing 'Grief and a Headhunter's Rage . . .' . . ." Reflecting further on death, rage and headhunting, my journal goes on to describe my wish for the Ilongot solution; they are much more in touch with reality than Christians. (p. 184)

Out of Rosaldo's reaction to his wife's death emerged his paper "Grief and a Headhunter's Rage" (1984). He was not able to enter into and understand the Ilongots' experience until he had been through an experience like theirs. Only then did he gain an emotional understanding of the headhunter's rage. When this occurred, he was able to grasp the meaning of the simple explanation the men gave for why they hunted heads after the deaths of loved ones.

The Lessons of Emotion

From Rosaldo's experience, we can learn several lessons. First, an observer cannot write meaningful interpretation until he or she has emotionally entered into and been part of the experiences he or she writes about. Second, readers cannot be expected to identify with and understand a set of written interpretations emotionally unless those interpretations are written in a way that elicits emotional identification and understanding. A reader cannot be expected to feel or understand something that the writer does not feel. Third, a writer can produce nonspurious emotional understandings only if he or she brings alive the world of lived experience in the pages of the text. Fourth, a writer cannot create emotional understandings if readers are not willing to enter into the writer's text and the world of lived experience he or she depicts.

CONCLUSION

In this chapter I have reviewed the various forms and types of interpretation. I have discussed the relationships among interpretation, description, and understanding, and I have stressed the central place of emotionality in the interpretive process. In Chapter 8, I turn to the main conclusions of this work.

8

Conclusion: On Interpretive Interactionism

This chapter reviews the essential features of the interpretive approach to the study of problematic experience and locates interpretive interactionism within the postmodern period of world history. The following topics are discussed: (a) the steps and phases of interpretation, (b) the structures of biographical experience, (c) the reading and writing of interpretation, (d) fiction and interpretation, and (e) interpretive interactionism in the postmodern period.

The basic topic that has guided the discussion in this volume, how to do interpretive interactionism as a mode of qualitative research, has served a double purpose. On the one hand, the structures of interpretive research have been illuminated. On the other, this inquiry has revealed the centrality of the study of those life experiences that radically alter the meanings persons give to themselves and their experiences. In this concluding chapter, I review and offer reflections on these two purposes. If interpretive sociology is to advance its standing in the human disciplines, then the basic elements of interpretive interactionism demand further elaboration and presentation.

INTERPRETATION

The subject matter of interpretive studies is biographically meaningful experience. Borrowing from James Joyce, I have used the term *epiphanies* to describe those interactional moments that leave positive and negative marks on people's lives. Often these moments are experienced as personal troubles that later become public issues (Mills, 1959). On other occasions, epiphanies are experienced in positive terms, as when Martin Luther King, Jr. heard an inner voice one night at his kitchen table and understood it to be the voice of Jesus Christ. The interpretive interactionist seeks out subjects who have experienced epiphanies. I have offered several examples of such experiences in this text, including murder, wife battering, seeking help for alcoholism, and experiencing the death of a loved one.

Steps to Interpretation

The interpretive process involves seven steps:

1. Framing the "how" question
2. Connecting personal troubles with public issues
3. Deconstructing the phenomenon of interest
4. Capturing the phenomenon
5. Bracketing the phenomenon
6. Construction the phenomenon
7. Contextualizing the phenomenon

I comment briefly below on step 3.

Deconstruction and Cultural Studies

As the "how" question takes shape, the researcher must work to free him- or herself of prior conceptions of the phenomenon being studied (Lindesmith, Strauss, & Denzin, 1999, p. 186). If the researcher is not successful in this, he or she will be trapped by those prior conceptions. To free him- or herself of those conceptions, the researcher must conduct a serious, critical, deconstructive reading of the existing scientific and commonsense literature on the problem.

The world of lived experience is shaped by cultural understandings and cultural texts. These texts often give meaning to problematic experiences. For example, movies that focus on alcoholism and problematic drinkers show viewers how alcoholic drinkers drink. Some of these films show how A.A. works. Others show alcoholics in treatment centers. Such films often speak to the lived experiences of alcoholics and their families (see Denzin, 1991).

Accordingly, a primary step in any interpretive study is the collection of the relevant cultural texts that represent the problematic experiences in question. The researcher must then subject these texts to a deconstructive reading. He or she must dissect the recurring images of the phenomenon found in the texts and must read the texts' semiotic, signifying structures. At the same time, the researcher should read the texts through the lens of feminist theory, in order to extract the images of women that exist within them. The texts will also presume particular pictures of work, money, and the economy; the researcher must identify and critique these conceptions. In deconstructing a cultural text, the researcher must identify the dominant meanings and codes in the text and then perform a subversive, or critical, reading of the text, exposing in the process its underlying values and assumptions.

BIOGRAPHICAL EXPERIENCE

Meaningful biographical experience occurs during turning-point interactional episodes. In these existentially problematic moments, human character is revealed and human lives are shaped, sometimes irrevocably. Some discussion of the structures of these moments and the experiences that flow from them is necessary.

Four Experiential Structures

It is possible to identify four major structures or types of existentially problematic moments, or epiphanies, in the lives of individuals. First are those moments that are major and touch every part of the fabric of a person's life. Their effects are immediate and long-term. Second are those epiphanies that represent eruptions, or reactions to events that have been going on for a long period of time. Third are those events that are minor yet symbolically representative of major problematic moments in a relationship. Fourth, and finally, are those episodes whose effects are immediate, but to which the individuals involved attach meanings only later, in retrospection and in the reliving of the events. I call these four structures of problematic experience, respectively, the major epiphany; the cumulative epiphany; the illuminative, minor epiphany; and the relived epiphany. (Of course, any epiphany can be relived and given new retrospective meaning.) These four types may build upon one another. For example, a given event may, at different phases in a person's or relationship's life, be first major, then minor, and then later relived. A cumulative epiphany will of course erupt into a major event in a person's life. Below, I offer examples of each type of epiphany.

The major epiphany. Recall once again the murder committed by the character Raskolnikov in Dostoyevsky's *Crime and Punishment.* In Chapter 2, I used Dostoyevsky's account of this event as an example of how thick description is written. Readers of *Crime and Punishment* know that this murder is a major, turning-point experience in Raskolnikov's life. It leads to his arrest, trial, imprisonment, and subsequent religious experience in a prison camp.

The cumulative epiphany. Recall Johnson and Ferraro's (1984) battered wife, who lived with her violent husband for years, until one day he put a gun to her head. On that day, she sued for separation of property and left her husband. This woman's turning-point experience did not just happen, it was the result of an accumulation of past experiences that culminated in a single moment.

The illuminative, minor epiphany. Consider the following interactional episode. Four persons are seated around a family kitchen table near a window that looks out on a bird feeder in the backyard. The individuals are Jack, a 55-year-old bachelor; his girlfriend, Shelly; Jack's mother, Mae; and Paul, a 47-year-old, recently divorced friend of Jack. Jack has brought his new girlfriend home to meet his mother. Paul has recently met Mae. Mae and Jack have been fighting for years over Jack's inability to settle down and become a respectable, married man. The following conversation was reported.

Mae: [Looking out the window] My word, that bird feeder's empty. Seems like it's always empty these days.

Jack: I'll fill it, Ma. No problem. Birdseed still where it always was?

Mae: Ya, now don't go and fill it more than halfway up. [Turning to Shelly and Paul, in front of Jack] He never listens to me. He always spills seed on the ground. He's just like a little boy.

[Jack goes out the back door, gets the birdseed from the woodshed, takes the sack of seed to the bird feeder, and, as the others watch through the window, pours seed into the feeder until it overflows.]

Mae: [Shouting through the window] You idiot, I said half full! Can't you remember anything!? [To Shelly and Paul] He never listens to me. It's always been like this. Why can't he do what I want him to?

This interaction between a mother and her son may be read as revealing underlying tensions and conflicts in their relationship. It is not a turning-point moment, but it brings to the surface and illuminates what has been, in the past, a break or rupture in the relationship. The son has refused to live his life as his mother wants him to. His refusal to follow her instructions on how to put birdseed in the bird feeder symbolically speaks to this rupture. It is a minor epiphany.

The relived epiphany. Finally, recall the story of the death of Michelle Rosaldo in 1981, noted in Chapter 7. Renato Rosaldo was still determining the meaning of the death of his wife 2 years after it happened. Her death was a major event in his life, and it led him to reinterpret his entire relationship to the field of anthropology.

Studying Epiphanies

As the investigator grounds his or her study in lived experience, he or she will observe major, cumulative, minor, and relived epiphanies. The researcher must, as much as possible, collect and study each of the above types of epiphanies within any interpretive investigation. Otherwise, he or she will be unable to produce a thickly described and thickly interpreted picture of problematic experience. This is what is involved in doing *existential ethnography*.

READING AND WRITING
INTERPRETATION

A brief analysis of the reading and writing of interpretation is appropriate at this point. This analysis must include discussion of readers, writers, texts, and systems of discourse. A *system of discourse* is a way of representing the world. A complex system of discourse is called a *discursive formation*. Systems of discourse are implemented through *discursive practices*. The standards of etiquette in the United States, for example, implement the ideologies of patriarchy. A *text* is part of a discursive system; the term can refer to any printed, visual, oral, or auditory (e.g., musical) statement that is available for reading, viewing, or hearing. Texts are always authored. They may be authored by ordinary, interacting individuals or professionally produced by scholars or professionals. A *reader* is a person who reads, hears, sees, and interprets a text. A reader may be an ordinary person, a professional, or a scholar. A *writer,* or author, is a person, agency, or institution who creates a text that is read, seen, or heard by others. An author may be an ordinary person telling another person about his or her life or a professional writer, such as an ethnographer, a sociologist, or a critic. Readers, writers, and texts exist within larger cultural, political, and ideological contexts (Barthes, 1967). A political, ideological process structures the creation of readers, writers, and texts.

Readers

Throughout the preceding chapters, I have argued that the writers of interpretive texts require willing readers. By this I mean that a reader must be willing to enter into the emotional fields of experience that are contained in a writer's text. Coleridge (1817/1973, p. 516) termed this the "willing suspension of disbelief"—that is, a readiness on the reader's part to trust and have faith in the writer. More is involved, however.

A reader brings meaning to and creates the text that he or she reads. This means that there is no absolute point or degree zero in a text (Barthes,

1953/1973). Three issues are involved in this assertion. First, texts are not unambiguous in their meanings. Readers bring to texts their own experiences with the experiences that are written about. Second, readers bring their own understandings and interpretations of the words that are used in texts. Third, as they emotionally and cognitively interact with texts, readers may be drawn to what they read, repulsed by it, or bored by it; they may disagree with it, not understand it, or completely accept it. Readers do not have neutral relationships to the texts that they read.

Here is the author of an oral text challenging his listeners. He is speaking at an A.A. meeting.

> You may not like what I'm about to say. You may hate me. But that's all right. I've lied. I've cheated, I've stolen things. I've been violent to people, once I broke a man's back because he wouldn't give me a hit. I don't care what you think, I'm here for me. (quoted in Denzin, 1987b, p. 191)

In this statement the speaker, as the writer or author of his own text, anticipates his audience's revulsion toward what he is about to say. He knows that there are no neutral listeners.

The following statement by a member of the group who heard this man speak confirms his prediction:

> What was he trying to do? Who does he think he is? Does he think he's unique? How long has he been in treatment anyway? When's he goin to learn to talk for himself and not for who he think's listen'n to him? I didn't believe him anyway. I have a lotta trouble with people like him. (p. 191)

Here the audience member, as the reader of an oral text, makes a judgment about the text and the speaker.

Readers constitute texts as they read and interact with those texts. This means that for any given reader, some texts are more readerly than others. Some readers prefer texts with thick descriptions that evoke emotional interpretations. Other readers like clear, minimalist, unambiguous, unemotional texts.

Writers and Texts

The texts that writers produce are shaped by language, ideology, gender, and myth, as well as by history, convention, and style.

Language

Language, of course, structures the process of writing. Words define the objects and the experiences that are written about. But language, with its syntactic and semantic structures (e.g., rules of sentence construction, rules of meaning), dictates what a writer can write. I can't call a cow a dog, for example, and convey to you that I am writing about a cow and not a dog. I cannot say, "Cow writing about am a I" and convince you that this is a sentence that states, "I am writing about a cow." The rules of language structure what I write and what you read and interpret.

Every word that I write, every object to which I refer, is already filled with meaning. If I write about experiences or epiphanies, you bring your own meanings (as I have noted above) to these words. If you consult a dictionary, you will find many different meanings for these two words. Words overflow with meaning. What writers write, then, is predetermined, in part, by what their language allows them to write. The same holds, of course, for readers.

Ideology

Barthes (1957/1972) reminds us that the culture- and knowledge-making institutions of a society, including the law, medicine, religion, the physical and the social sciences, the humanities, the arts, and the mass media, produce and reproduce knowledge and records of social events that structure and give meaning to everyday life. These representations, records, and texts often lend a sense of "naturalness" to the events that have been recorded and written about. In the process, they "dress up a reality which, even though it is the one we live in, is undoubtedly determined by history" (Barthes, 1957/1972, p. 11). By displaying events and happenings as natural occurrences, texts confuse nature and history, for "what-goes-without-saying" (Barthes, 1957/1972, p. 11) in a display or text is ideologically shaped. This means that one cannot read these works as "literal" representations of the social situations to which they refer. They are ideological representations of the social, and they reflect the biases and prejudices of their producers.

Gender

The representations in texts often reflect a patriarchal or male interpretive bias. They view the social world through the male gaze and present only the male voice. They often equate masculinity with objectivity and femininity with subjectivity. In the process, they "obscure the patriarchal bias at the core of science" (Cook & Fonow, 1986, p. 6). Like myth, such texts have reproduced the gender stratification systems of postmodern society.

Myth

The representations that social scientists write may be likened to myths. A myth is a text that is based on an everyday phenomenon. A myth tells a story that offers or contains an explanation of some fact, phenomenon, or event. It is presented in readable language that makes the explanation seem sensible, natural, orderly, and understandable. Myths present "truths" about reality.

I have given numerous examples of myth in earlier chapters. In Chapter 6, I quoted from Collins's (1975) interpretation of the "rating and dating complex" in American society. In that statement, Collins offers an explanation for the presence of force in the dating system. He implicitly suggests that some women allow themselves to be raped if they think marriage to a desirable mate will be the outcome. This is a mythical statement. It presents accounts of things and happenings.

Myth often distorts and reproduces biases and prejudices that exist within the larger culture. Collins's account of force in the dating relationship can be read as his saying that women encourage men to take advantage of them sexually. Taken to its extreme, this interpretation holds women responsible for being raped. It must be noted that all myth is ideological. Myth either supports the status quo or challenges the current arrangement of things in the social world. Myth on the right supports the status quo. Myth on the left often calls for radical social change (Barthes, 1957/1972, pp. 145-150).

History, Convention, and Style

More than language, ideology, gender, and myth shape what goes into a text. Convention and style also influence what is written. *Convention* refers to established ways or modes of presentation. *Style* refers to variations within a convention and is often associated with the work of particular persons or groups. Historically, in the social sciences two dominant writing conventions have prevailed: the scientific article and the humanistic essay. The scientific article builds on the social science myth of objectivity. It is often filled with such terms as *hypothesis, hypothesis testing, reliability, validity, generalization,* and *standard error.* First-person statements are typically absent. The text is written as if it objectively maps the empirical reality under inspection. Within the conventional structure of the scientific article, individual authors establish their own styles of presentation.

The humanistic essay is often written in the first person. It extends the myth of subjectivity and the importance of studying human subjects. It lacks the rigorous organization of the scientific article and avoids terms such as *hypothesis testing* and *reliability*. This convention, as used in the social sciences, draws the writer (and the reader) closer to literary styles of writing.

Styles of Writing Interpretation

Interpretive writing is located, of course, within the humanistic writing tradition in the social sciences. In the past decade, there has been a proliferation of interpretive writing styles, or what Richardson (2000) calls "creative analytic practices." In Chapter 7, I identified several styles or ways of writing interpretation, including monologic, dialogic, polyphonic, analytic, factual-descriptive, and interpretive-narrative styles. Now I want to make matters slightly more complicated by introducing three additional writing styles. I call these *mainstream realism, interpretive realism,* and *descriptive realism* (see Rabinow, 1986).

Mainstream realism. Mainstream realism assumes that the author of a text can give an objective accounting or portrayal of the realities of a group or an individual. It attempts to capture the objective elements of a culture and social structure. For example, a mainstream realist researcher might use traditional concepts such as kinship, economic and religious systems, norms and values, deviance, and social control. He or she would then map these structures onto the experiences observed. Mainstream realism assumes that structures such as those found in concepts like kinship and political system in fact exist in the group being studied. It also assumes that an "objective" reading of these structures can be given. Mainstream realism leads to the production of monologic, analytic, interpretive texts (see the discussion of Collins, 1975, above).

Interpretive realism. Interpretive realism describes that mode of writing in which the author presumes to be able to interpret the realities of other people. Clifford Geertz is known for producing such texts. The observer's interpretations displace those of the native. Interpretive realist texts often have the flavor of "I was there and this is what I experienced." However, this experiential tone is filtered through the experiences of the observer, not the native.

Descriptive realism. In descriptive realism the writer attempts to allow the world being interpreted to interpret itself. Here the writer employs the strategy of using multiple voices to speak from his or her text. In the following extract, the film critic Michiko Kakutani (1987) is discussing John Huston's film *The Dead,* which is based on James Joyce's short story of the same title. Kakutani argues that Joyce's early stories introduced Huston to the possibilities of realism. He quotes Wieland Schulz-Keil, one of the producers of *The Dead,* who in a conversation stated that perhaps Huston

> learned from Joyce that a story should not attempt to interpret life, but should describe an order and an interpretation arising from life itself. Joyce and Huston show views of life as they emerge from their stories' characters. These interpretations can be discerned in the thought of the characters, their consciousness and . . . in their words and actions. It is not one view but many that overlap, complement and contradict each other. This is realism in action. It explains . . . the absence of a homogeneous, identifiable style in the work of the two authors. The style changes with the characters whose view of life . . . is revealed in any instance. (pp. 1, 50)

Descriptive realism is dialogic and polyphonic. It tells a person's story in his or her own words. It allows interpretation to emerge from the stories that are told. It reveals the conflictual, contradictory nature of lived experience and suggests that no single story or interpretation will fully capture the problematic events that have been studied. Descriptive realism assumes that reasonable, plausible, workable theories and accounts of experience can be given by those persons who have experienced the event or events in question. After all, it is their lives that the writer is telling about.

Here is an example from Vincent Crapanzano's 1980 book *Tuhami: Portrait of a Moroccan.* Tuhami, a Moroccan tile maker, told Crapanzano stories about his life that were fantasies, made-up accounts of experiences that could not have "really" happened. Yet Tuhami believed them and acted as if they were real. Consider the following:

> That is what I told you yesterday. . . . When I dream, I dream of things that are true, I dream and fight. I never call to anyone but Allah. . . . Today I find that my limbs are strong. . . . When you burn spices, it strangles the others at the neck. . . . I'll have my freedom because I saw Mme Jolan in my room. The moment I woke up, I saw her. (p. 172)

Tuhami believes that what he dreams is real. He lives his life in terms of experiences like this. He is able to distinguish between the "reality" of personal history and the "truth" of autobiography (Crapanzano, 1980, p. 5).

The reality of personal history refers to some correspondence between a text or narrative and some set of external, observable experiences. The truth of an autobiography "resides within the text itself without any regard to any external criteria save, perhaps the I of the narrator" (Crapanzano, 1980, p. 5). Descriptive realism attempts to capture autobiographical narratives (personal experience stories and self-stories). These stories may or may not be true in any objectively verifiable sense. They have meaning for and structure the life experiences of their narrators. This brings me, finally, to the topic of fiction and interpretation.

FICTION AND INTERPRETATION

Fiction, usually a story or narrative, is something made up out of experience. A fiction is not opposed to something that is true (Clifford, 1986, p. 6). It is fashioned out of something that was thought, imagined, acted out, or experienced. All interpretation is fictional in the sense that it involves either the observer's or the subject's accounting of what has occurred, or of what something means. Fictions are true, but only within the stories that contain them. If something can be imagined, it is real (Denzin, 1984a, p. 211; Sartre, 1948, pp. 165-166). Tuhami's fictions, his dreams and his fantasies, are true—that is, they are true for him. These are the only truths that descriptive, realist, existential ethnographers seek.

The above assertion that all interpretation is fictional carries with it five implications for writers of interpretation. First, writers of interpretation must free themselves from the erroneous preconception that they do not write fictions. Second, such writers must learn how to experiment with modes of writing that are not tied to mainstream and interpretive realist criteria of evaluation. Third, they must learn to listen to the "truthful, fictional" stories that persons tell. Fourth, they must learn how to hear these stories for what they are—meaningful accounts of existentially problematic experience. Fifth, they must experiment with alternative ways of presenting interpretation, including through films, novels, plays, songs, music, poems, dance, paintings, photography, sculptures, pottery, toolmaking, and architecture. Each of these representational forms speaks to the problem of presenting and doing interpretation. By experimenting with different forms, the interpreter enlarges his or her interpretive horizon. In so doing, he or she opens wider the windows of interpretation that look out onto the worlds he or she has studied. This means that interpretive interactionists must direct their studies to life in the postmodern period.

INTERPRETIVE INTERACTIONISM
IN THE POSTMODERN PERIOD

"All classic social scientists have been concerned with the salient characteristics of their time" (Mills, 1959, p. 165; see also Lemert, 1997b, p. 161). This means that social scientists have been preoccupied with how history and human nature are being made within their own historical moments. They have been concerned with the variety and types of men, women, and children who have prevailed in any given historical moment (Mills, 1959, p. 165).

Human history can be divided into at least four epochs: antiquity, the Middle Ages, the modern age, and now the fourth epoch, or the postmodern period (Mills, 1959, p. 166). The last two decades of the 20th century and the first decade of the 21st century have found us in the middle of the late postmodern period, which began after World War II. This is the age of multinational corporations, satellite communication systems, an interdependent world economy, racism and racial injustice, single-parent families, day-care children, working mothers, the "graying" of America, the threat of nuclear annihilation, environmental destruction, increasing domination of biomedical technologies, problems with drug and alcohol addiction, and armed confrontations in the Middle East, Central America, and South Africa.

The postmodern age is one in which advertising and the mass media, especially television and the Internet, have gained ever greater control over human lives and human experience. This is an age in which problematic experiences are given meaning in the mass media. Social objects have become commodities. Human experience and social relationships have also become commodities, as anyone who scans the travel sections of the Sunday newspapers, with their supplements on holiday tours, can quickly confirm.

It is an age marked by nostalgia for the past. Extreme self-interest and personal gain, coupled with the ostentatious display of material possessions, characterize the lifestyles of many today. At the same time, there are massive anxieties at the level of the personal and the social. According to some sources, one in three American adults is now seeking psychotherapy or other forms of professional help for individual problems. This is an age of personal unrest in which individual, family, sexual, leisure, and work experiences are becoming more and more problematic (Lemert, 1997b, p. 159).

Interpretive interactionism in the late postmodern period is committed to understanding how this historical moment universalizes itself in the lives of interacting individuals. Each person and each relationship studied is assumed to be a universal singular, or a single instance of the universal themes that structure the postmodern period. Each person is touched by the mass media, by alienation, by the economy, by the new family and child-care systems, by the increasing technologizing of the social world, and by the threat of nuclear annihilation. Interpretive interactionism fits itself to the relation between the individual and society, to the nexus of biography and society. Interpretive interactionism attempts to show how individual troubles and problems become public issues. In the discovery of this nexus, it attempts to bring alive the existentially problematic, often hidden, and private experiences that give meaning to everyday life as it is lived in this moment in history.

To make the invisible more visible to others is, after all, a major goal of the interpreter (Merleau-Ponty, 1968). This means that we want to capture the stories of everyday persons as they tell about the joys, the agonies, the emotional experiences, the small and the large victories, the traumas, the fears, the anxieties, the dreams, the fantasies, and the hopes in their lives. We want to make those stories available to others. This is an ongoing interpretive project. Our challenge is clear, to represent and perform the many different ways in which humans make and inscribe history, but not under circumstances of their own choosing (see Willis & Trondman, 2000, p. 6).

Ben Agger (2000) says that we want a good sociology that is "unashamed in its advocacy" (p. 257). This is a public sociology that addresses "social problems accessibly" (p. 257) and does so with good writing. But there is more to good writing than just this. In 1972, Laurel Richardson was almost killed in an automobile accident. Two years later, she returned to her writing table. Speaking of the centrality of writing in her life, she states, "Writing was the method through which I constituted the world and reconstituted myself" (Richardson, 1999, p. 89). She learned that she was "writing for her life" (p. 89). We are writing for our lives, and for the lives of others as well, for our words matter.

To repeat what I said at the end of Chapter 2, citing C. Wright Mills and William Faulkner, the sociologist's voice must speak to the terrible and magnificent world of human experience in the first years of the 21st century. And so here at the end, in the seventh moment, at the beginning of the 21st century, we confront the pressing demand to show how the practices of critical, interpretive qualitative research can help change the world in positive ways. That is what this book has been all about.

Glossary

Account: An explanation of a set of actions or experiences.

Analytic interpretation: Imposes an abstract, often causal scheme on a set of experiences or events; usually derives from a scientific theory.

Biographical experience: Experience that shapes a person's life; how reality presents itself to consciousness (Bruner, 1986, p. 6); the subject matter of interpretive interactionism. *See also* Problematic experience.

Biography: A written account or history of the life of an individual; the art of writing such accounts.

Bracketing: Isolating the key, essential features of the processes under inspection.

Capture: Securing instances of the phenomenon being studied.

Cause: A narrative accounting of a set of actions or experiences; may be commonsense or scientific.

Construction: Follows bracketing, involves putting the key elements of a phenomenon back together again, in temporal order; leads to contextualization.

Contextualization: Relocation of bracketed phenomenon back in the worlds of lived experience.

Convention: An established mode of presentation; may be humanistic or scientific. There are styles within conventions.

Cultural studies: A field of inquiry that takes as its subject matter the culture-making institutions of a society and their productions of meaning. Interpretive studies examine the problematic lived experiences shaped by these culture-making institutions.

Deconstruction: Critical analysis and interpretation of prior studies and representations of the phenomenon in question.

Description: The art of describing, giving an account of anything in words. Types: thick and thin.

Descriptive realism: Allowing the world studied to interpret itself; leads to dialogic and polyphonic texts.

Dialogic interpretation: An interpretation that is a dialogue between the observer and those studied, usually multivoiced, or polyphonic. Contrasted to monologic interpretation, which suppresses the voices of those studied.

Engulfing: Building an interpretation that includes all that is known to be relevant about a phenomenon; always incomplete.

Epiphany: Moment of problematic experience that illuminates personal character and often signifies a turning point in a person's life. Types: major, minor, illuminative, relived.

Ethnography: The study of lived experiences, involving description and interpretation.

Existential ethnography: That mode of ethnography that collects and studies problematic, turning-point experiences in the lives of ordinary people.

Expression: How individual and interactional experience is framed and articulated. Expressions of experience are symbolic and include drama, performances, ritual, and storytelling (see Bruner, 1986, pp. 6-7).

Feminist critique: Locates gender asymmetry at the center of the social world, including the world of social inquiry. There is no gender-free knowledge. The same argument holds for race and ethnicity as processes that also shape inquiry and experience in basic ways.

Fiction: A story or narrative made up out of experience. Fictions are always true within the stories that contain them. All interpretation is mythical and fictional.

Gloss: A superficial, partial rendering or accounting of a phenomenon. Types: everyday and scientific.

Hermeneutic circle: All interpreters are caught in the circle of interpretation. It is impossible to be free of interpretations or to conduct "purely" objective studies.

Ideology: An accounting of the way things are and should be, typically political. Involves the manipulation of ideas about the world we live in.

Idiographic research: Research that treats each individual as a *universal singular* and seeks to study experience from within. Also called *emic.* To be contrasted to *etic,* nomothetic studies that attempt to generalize across subjects.

Informed reader: A reader who knows the language spoken in a story, who knows the biography of the storyteller, is able to take the teller's point of view, has had the experiences told about in the story, is willing to take responsibility for his or her interpretations of the story, and is knowledgeable in the full range of interpretive theories that could be brought to bear upon the story in question.

Interaction: Symbolically taking the perspective of another and acting on that perspective. Interaction is always emergent.

Interactional slice: An interactional sequence that has been recorded.

Interactional text: Text that occurs whenever an individual is located in a social situation.

Interpret: To explain the meaning of, to translate into intelligible or familiar terms. Leads to understanding.

Interpretation: The act of interpreting. Creates the conditions for understanding; may be emotional, cognitive, spurious, or authentic. Interpretation is a temporal process and is always symbolic. Types: thin, thick, native, observer, analytic, monologic, dialogic, polyphonic, descriptive-contextual, relational-interactional. All interpretations should be relational, interactional, contextual, dialogic, and polyphonic.

Interpreter: One who interprets or translates meaning for others. Types: native and scientific, or well-informed experts.

Interpretive: Explaining the meaning of; the act of interpreting or conferring meaning.

Interpretive biographical method: A method that utilizes personal experience narratives, self-stories, and personal histories.

Interpretive evaluation: Interpretive, naturalistic, program evaluation, policy-making research that makes the investigator an advocate or partisan for those served by applied programs.

Interpretive interactionism: The point of view that illuminates and confers meaning on problematic symbolic interaction. Seeks to use a concept-free mode of discourse, based on first-order concepts from lived experience.

Interpretive process: Involves six steps, or phases: framing the research question, deconstructing the phenomenon, capturing the phenomenon, bracketing the phenomenon, constructing the phenomenon, and contextualizing the phenomenon.

Interpretive realism: A mode of writing in which the author presumes to be able to interpret the realities of other people. Closely related to mainstream realism, usually associated with monologic texts.

Interpretive studies: The interpretive project that takes as its subject matter biographically meaningful experience.

Interpretive theory: A theory, interpretation, or accounting of a set of experiences; may be local or scientific.

Issue: A personal trouble that becomes a public problem.

Lay theory: An interpretive account of experience developed by the person having the experience.

Life: The biographical experiences of a named person. A life has two levels, the surface and the deep.

Lived experience: The world of actual experience.

Mainstream realism: A writing style that attempts to report on the realities of a group "objectively."

Meaning: What an experience means to a person, defined in terms of intentions and consequences. Meaning is always triadic, involving interactions among a person, an object, and action taken toward the object. Meaning is interactional, interpretive, open-ended, often ambiguous, inconclusive, and conflictual.

Myth: A text, usually a story, that presents "truths" about reality, usually ideologically shaped. May be on the left or on the right, and may be produced by ordinary people or by professional observers of society.

Narrative: A story that has a plot and a beginning, middle, and end.

Narrator: A person who tells a story.

Naturalism: The location of inquiry in the natural worlds of everyday social experience and the use of methods that respect this world.

Participant observation: The researcher's observation and participation in the worlds of lived experience he or she is studying. Involves learning how to listen, see, and talk within the worlds being studied.

Personal experience narrative: A story that relates the self of the teller to a significant set of personal experiences that have already occurred.

Personal history: Reconstruction of a life based on interviews, conversations, self-stories, and personal experience narratives.

Postmodern: Two meanings: life since World War II and a mode of discourse that seeks to write life experiences in the postmodern period.

Problematic experience: Epiphanies or moments of crisis in a person's life.

Problematic interaction: Interactional experiences that give primary meaning to a person's life.

Progressive-regressive method: A method that seeks to locate and understand a class of subjects within a given historical moment. Moves forward to the conclusion of a set of experiences and then backward to the historical, cultural, and biographical conditions that moved the subject to take or experience the actions being studied. Also called *critical interpretive method.*

Pure interpretation: Interpretation for the purposes of building meaningful interpretations and understandings of social, cultural, and biographical problematics.

Reader: One who reads, hears, or sees and interprets a text.

Realism: The relationship between a text and the world of lived experience. Produces three writing styles: mainstream realism, interpretive realism, and descriptive realism.

Reality: The world of lived experience.

Research question: The question that defines the subject of research. Always phrased as a "how" question, not a "why" question.

Self-story: A narrative that creates and interprets a structure of experience that is being told about. The self of the teller is at the center of the story.

Semiotic analysis: A method for reading the meanings of words and signs within narrative and interactional texts. Semiotic analysis directs attention to the codes, metaphors, and metonymies that organize the text and suggests that texts are structured in terms of oppositions (e.g., male versus female). Any text contains multiple, often contradictory meanings and messages that a semiotic analysis can help to disclose.

Social type: An individual who represents through his or her actions a typical way of acting in a social situation.

Style: A variation within a writing or speaking convention.

Symbolic interaction: Human interactional experience mediated by language and symbols.

Temporal mapping: Connecting individuals to social situations. Includes determining temporal sequencing and the location of the situations where persons come together. Focuses on who does what with whom, when, and where.

Text: Any printed, visual, oral, or auditory statement that is available for reading, viewing, or hearing. Readers create texts as they read them. The meaning of a text is always indefinite. Readers, writers, and texts are shaped by the forces of language, ideology, gender, and myth, as well as history, convention, and style.

Theory: An interpretive structure that renders a set of experiences meaningful and understandable. May be lay or professional; always derives from the cultural understandings of a group.

Thick description: Description that captures the meanings and experiences that have occurred in a problematic situation. Reports meanings, intentions, history, biography, and relevant relational, interactional, and situational processes in a rich, dense, detailed manner. Creates the conditions for interpretation and understanding. Contrasted to thin description, which is only factual. Types: micro, macrohistorical, biographical, situational, relational, interactional, intrusive, incomplete, glossed, purely descriptive, descriptive, and interpretive.

Thick interpretation: Builds on thick description; attempts to take the reader to the heart of the experience being studied.

Thin description: Description that lacks detail; a simple reporting of acts, independent of intentions or the circumstances that organize them; a gloss. Types: everyday glosses, social science glosses, typified.

Troubles: Problems that occur within the immediate worlds of experience of individuals. Personal troubles are often translated into public issues and into institutional responses intended to deal with them. Examples include wife battering, rape, problem drinking, alcoholism, drug addiction, and AIDS.

Understanding: Comprehension or grasping of the meaning of an interpreted phenomenon; may be emotional, or cognitive, or both. Understanding is an interactional, emotional process, involving shared experiences; the process may produce spurious or authentic understanding. The goal of interpretation is to build authentic, shareable understandings of the phenomenon under investigation. Also called *verisimilitude.*

Universal singular: Term attached to the concept that every person is a singular instance of the universal themes that structure his or her moment in history.

Writer: A person, agency, or institution that creates a text that is read, seen, or heard by others. A writer may be an ordinary person or a professional (e.g., an ethnographer, sociologist, anthropologist, novelist, painter). Also called *author.*

References

Abu-Lughod, Lila. (1997). The interpretation of culture(s) after television. *Reflections, 59,* 109-134.

Abu-Lughod, Lila. (2001). Locating ethnography. *Ethnography, 1,* 261-267.

Adler, Patricia A., & Adler, Peter. (1987). *Membership roles in field research.* Newbury Park, CA: Sage.

Agger, Ben. (2000). *Public sociology: From social facts to literary acts.* New York: Rowman & Littlefield.

Alcoholics Anonymous World Services. (1976). *Alcoholics Anonymous* (3rd ed.). New York: Author.

Alcoholics Anonymous World Services. (1989). *Twelve steps and twelve traditions.* New York: Author. (Original work published 1953)

Allport, Gordon W. (1942). *The use of personal documents in psychological science.* New York: Social Science Research Council.

Angrosino, Michael V., & Mays de Pérez, Kimberly A. (2000). Rethinking observation: From method to context. In Norman K. Denzin & Yvonna S. Lincoln (Eds.), *Handbook of qualitative research* (2nd ed., pp. 673-702). Thousand Oaks, CA: Sage.

Appadurai, Arjun. (1991). Global ethnoscapes: Notes and queries for a transnational anthropology. In Richard G. Fox (Ed.), *Recapturing anthropology: Working in the present* (pp. 191-210). Santa Fe, NM: School of American Research Press.

Appadurai, Arjun. (1996). *Modernity at large: Cultural dimensions of globalization.* Minneapolis: University of Minnesota Press.

Athens, Lonnie H. (1984a). Blumer's method of naturalistic inquiry: A critical examination. In Norman K. Denzin (Ed.), *Studies in symbolic interaction: A research annual* (Vol. 5, pp. 241-257). Greenwich, CT: JAI.

Athens, Lonnie H. (1984b). Scientific criteria for evaluating qualitative studies. In Norman K. Denzin (Ed.), *Studies in symbolic interaction: A research annual* (Vol. 5, pp. 259-268). Greenwich, CT: JAI.

Bakhtin, Mikhail M. (1981). *The dialogic imagination: Four essays* (Michael Holquist, Ed.; Michael Holquist & C. Emerson, Trans.). Austin: University of Texas Press.

Barthes, Roland. (1967). *Elements of semiology.* New York: Hill & Wang,

Barthes, Roland. (1972). *Mythologies* (A. Lavers, Trans.). New York: Hill & Wang.

Barthes, Roland. (1973). *Writing degree zero.* New York: Hill & Wang. (Original work published 1953)

Baudrillard, Jean. (1983). *Simulations.* New York: Semiotext(e).

Becker, Howard S. (1967a). Introduction. In Howard S. Becker (Ed.), *Social problems: A modern approach* (pp. 1-31). New York: John Wiley.

Becker, Howard S. (1967b). Whose side are we on? *Social Problems, 14,* 239-247.

Becker, Howard S. (1973). *Outsiders.* New York: Free Press.

Becker, Howard S. (1986). *Doing things together: Selected papers.* Evanston, IL: Northwestern University Press.

Becker, Howard S. (2001). Response to the manifesto. *Ethnography, 1,* 257-260.

Becker, Howard S., & Horowitz, Irving Louis. (1986). Radical politics and sociological observation: Observations on methodology and ideology. In Howard S. Becker, *Doing things together: Selected papers* (pp. 83-102). Evanston, IL: Northwestern University Press.

Benhabib, Seyla. (1992). *Situating the self: Gender, community and postmodernism in contemporary ethics.* New York: Routledge.

Bertaux-Wiame, Isabelle. (1981). The life history approach to the study of internal migration. In Daniel Bertaux (Ed.), *Biography and society: The life history approach in the social sciences* (pp. 249-266). Beverly Hills, CA: Sage.

Beverley, John. (2000). Testimonio, subalternity, and narrative authority. In Norman K. Denzin & Yvonna S. Lincoln (Eds.), *Handbook of qualitative research* (2nd ed., pp. 555-565). Thousand Oaks, CA: Sage.

Birringer, Johannes H. (1991). *Theatre, theory, postmodernism.* Bloomington: Indiana University Press.

Blumer, Herbert. (1969). *Symbolic interactionism: Perspective and method.* Englewood Cliffs, NJ: Prentice Hall.

Bottomore, Tom. (1984). *The Frankfurt school.* London: Tavistock.

Brady, Ivan. (2000). Anthropological poetics. In Norman K. Denzin & Yvonna S. Lincoln (Eds.), *Handbook of qualitative research* (2nd ed., pp. 949-979). Thousand Oaks, CA: Sage.

Branaman, Ann. (1997). Goffman's social theory. In Charles Lemert & Ann Branaman (Eds.), *The Goffman reader* (pp. xvi-lxxxii). Malden, MA: Blackwell.

Bruner, Edward M. (1986). Experience and its expressions. In Victor W. Turner & Edward M. Bruner (Eds.), *The anthropology of experience* (pp. 3-30). Urbana: University of Illinois Press.

Bruner, Edward M. (1989). Tourism, creativity, and authenticity. In Norman K. Denzin (Ed.), *Studies in symbolic interaction: A research annual* (Vol. 10, pp. 109-114). Greenwich, CT: JAI.

Bruner, Edward M. (1996). Abraham Lincoln as authentic reproduction: A critique of postmodernism. *American Anthropologist, 96,* 397-415.

Butler, Judith. (1990). *Gender trouble: Feminism and the subversion of identity.* New York: Routledge.

Butler, Judith. (1997). *Excitable speech: A politics of the performative.* New York: Routledge.

Butler, Judith. (1999). Revisiting bodies and pleasures. *Theory, Culture & Society, 16,* 11-20.

Carey, James W. (1995). The press, public opinion, and public discourse. In Theodore L. Glasser & Charles T. Salmon (Eds.), *Public opinion and the communication of consent* (pp. 380-402). New York: Guilford.

Carspecken, Phil Frances. (1996). *Critical ethnography in educational research: A theoretical and practical guide.* New York: Routledge.

Chandler, Raymond. (1995). Twelve notes on the mystery story. In Raymond Chandler, *Later novels and other writings* (pp. 1004-1011). New York: Penguin.

Charity, Arthur. (1995). *Doing public journalism.* New York: Guilford.

Charmaz, Kathy. (2000). Grounded theory: Objectivist and constructivist methods. In Norman K. Denzin & Yvonna S. Lincoln (Eds.), *Handbook of qualitative research* (2nd ed., pp. 509-535). Thousand Oaks, CA: Sage.

Cho, Joo-Hyun. (1987). *A social phenomenological understanding of family violence: The case of Korea.* Unpublished doctoral dissertation, University of Illinois, Urbana, Department of Sociology.

Cho, Joo-Hyun. (1988). *Battered wives: Violence and ressentiment in the Korean family.* New York: Aldine de Gruyter.

Christians, Clifford G. (2000). Ethics and politics in qualitative research. In Norman K. Denzin & Yvonna S. Lincoln (Eds.), *Handbook of qualitative research* (2nd ed., pp. 133-155). Thousand Oaks, CA: Sage.

Christians, Clifford G., Ferre, John P., & Fackler, P. Mark. (1993). *Good news: Social ethics and the press.* New York: Oxford University Press.

Clifford, James. (1986). Introduction: Partial truths. In James Clifford & George E. Marcus (Eds.), *Writing culture: The poetics and politics of ethnography* (pp. 1-26). Berkeley: University of California Press.

Clough, Patricia Ticineto. (1994). *Feminist thought: Desire, power and academic discourse.* Cambridge, MA: Blackwell.

Clough, Patricia Ticineto. (1998). *The end(s) of ethnography: From realism to social criticism* (2nd ed.). New York: Peter Lang.

Coffey, Amanda. (1999). *The ethnographic self.* London: Sage.

Cohen-Cruz, Jan. (1998). General introduction. In Jan Cohen-Cruz (Ed.), *Radical street performance: An international anthology* (pp. 1-6). New York: Routledge.

Coleridge, Samuel Taylor. (1973). Biographia literaria. In William Heath (Ed.), *Major British poets of the romantic period.* New York: Macmillan. (Original work published 1817)

Collins, Patricia Hill. (1990). *Black feminist thought: Knowledge, consciousness, and the politics of empowerment.* New York: Routledge, Chapman & Hall.

Collins, Randall. (1975). *Conflict sociology: Toward an explanatory science.* New York: Academic Press.

Conquergood, Dwight. (1985). Performing as a moral act: Ethical dimensions of the ethnography of performance. *Literature in Performance, 5,* 1-13.

Conquergood, Dwight. (1998). Beyond the text: Toward a performative cultural politics. In Sheron J. Dailey (Ed.), *The future of performance studies: Visions and revisions* (pp. 25-36). Annandale, VA: National Communication Association.

Cook, Judith A., & Fonow, Mary Margaret. (1986). Knowledge and women's interests: Issues of epistemology and methodology in feminist sociological research. *Sociological Inquiry, 56,* 2-27.

Couch, Carl J. (1984). *Constructing civilizations.* Greenwich, CT: JAI.

Couch, Carl J. (1988). Towards the isolation of elements of social structures. In Norman K. Denzin (Ed.), *Studies in symbolic interaction: A research annual* (Vol. 10). Greenwich, CT: JAI.

Cowley, Malcolm. (1967). Introduction. In William Faulkner, *The portable Faulkner reader* (Rev. ed., Malcolm Cowley, Ed.). New York: Viking.

Crapanzano, Vincent. (1980). *Tuhami: Portrait of a Moroccan.* Chicago: University of Chicago Press.

Crapanzano, Vincent. (1986). Heremes' dilemma: The masking of subversion in ethnographic description. In James Clifford & George E. Marcus (Eds.), *Writing culture: The poetics and politics of ethnography* (pp. 51-76). Berkeley: University of California Press.

Creswell, John W. (1998). *Qualitative inquiry and research design: Choosing among five traditions.* Thousand Oaks, CA: Sage.

Culler, Jonathan. (1981). *The pursuit of signs: Semiotics, literature, deconstruction.* Ithaca, NY: Cornell University Press.

Dash, Leon. (1997). *Rosa Lee: A mother and her family in urban America.* New York: Penguin.

Davis, Angela Y. (1998). *Blues legacies and black feminism: Gertrude Ma Rainey, Bessie Smith, and Billie Holiday.* New York: Pantheon.

Dawson, Patrick. (1996). Not another fish story from occupied Montana. In Rick Newby & Susan Hunger (Eds.), *Writing Montana: Literature under the big sky* (pp. 10-23). Helena: Montana Center for the Book.

Degh, Linda. (1995). *Narratives in society: A performer-centered study of narration.* Bloomington: Indiana University Press.

Denzin, Norman K. (1970). *The research act in sociology.* Chicago: Aldine.

Denzin, Norman K. (1978). *The research act: A theoretical introduction to sociological methods* (2nd ed.). New York: McGraw-Hill.

Denzin, Norman K. (1983). Interpretive interactionism. In Gareth Morgan (Ed.), *Beyond method: Strategies for social research* (pp. 129-146). Beverly Hills, CA: Sage.

Denzin, Norman K. (1984a). *On understanding emotion.* San Francisco: Jossey-Bass.

Denzin, Norman K. (1984b). Toward a phenomenology of domestic, family violence. *American Journal of Sociology, 90,* 483-513.

Denzin, Norman K. (1987a). *The alcoholic self.* Newbury Park, CA: Sage.

Denzin, Norman K. (1987b). *The recovering alcoholic.* Newbury Park, CA: Sage.

Denzin, Norman K. (1987c). *Treating alcoholism.* Newbury Park, CA: Sage.

Denzin, Norman K. (1989a). *Interpretive biography.* Newbury Park, CA: Sage.

Denzin, Norman K. (1989b). *The research act: A theoretical introduction to sociological methods* (3rd ed.). Englewood Cliffs, NJ: Prentice Hall.

Denzin, Norman K. (1991). *Hollywood shot by shot: Film and the American alcoholic.* New York: Aldine de Gruyter.

Denzin, Norman K. (1992). *Symbolic interactionism and cultural studies.* Malden, MA: Blackwell.

Denzin, Norman K. (1997). *Interpretive ethnography: Ethnographic practices for the 21st century.* Thousand Oaks, CA: Sage.

Denzin, Norman K. (1998). Narratives of the self, co-dependency and the inner child: Emotionality, meaning and gender in a cyberspace community. In Gillian Bendelow & Simon J. Williams (Eds.), *Emotions in social life: Critical themes and contemporary issues* (pp. 97-119). London: Routledge.

Denzin, Norman K. (1999a). Cybertalk and the method of instances. In Steve G. Jones (Ed.), *Doing Internet research: Critical issues and methods for examining the Net* (pp. 130-142). Thousand Oaks, CA: Sage.

Denzin, Norman K. (1999b). Performing Montana. In Barry Glassner & Rosanna Hertz (Eds.), *Qualitative sociology as everyday life* (pp. 147-158). Thousand Oaks, CA: Sage.

Denzin, Norman K. (2000a). The practices and politics of interpretation. In Norman K. Denzin & Yvonna S. Lincoln (Eds.), *Handbook of qualitative research* (2nd ed., pp. 897-922). Thousand Oaks, CA: Sage.

Denzin, Norman K. (2000b). Rock Creek history. *Symbolic Interaction, 23,* 71-81.

Denzin, Norman K. (2001). *Reading race: Hollywood and the cinema of racial violence.* London: Sage.

Denzin, Norman K., Fields, A. Belden, Feinberg, Walter, & Roberts, Nicole. (1997). Remembering and forgetting recent racial politics. *Taboo: Journal of Culture and Education, 2,* 191-208.

Denzin, Norman K., & Lincoln, Yvonna S. (Eds.). (1994). *Handbook of qualitative research.* Thousand Oaks, CA: Sage.

Denzin, Norman K., & Lincoln, Yvonna S. (Eds.). (2000a). *Handbook of qualitative research* (2nd ed.). Thousand Oaks, CA: Sage.

Denzin, Norman K., & Lincoln, Yvonna S. (2000b). Introduction: The discipline and practice of qualitative research. In Norman K. Denzin & Yvonna S. Lincoln (Eds.), *Handbook of qualitative research* (2nd ed., pp. 1-28). Thousand Oaks, CA: Sage.

Denzin, Norman K., & Lincoln, Yvonna S. (2000c). Preface. In Norman K. Denzin & Yvonna S. Lincoln (Eds.), *Handbook of qualitative research* (2nd ed., pp. ix-xx). Thousand Oaks, CA: Sage.

Derrida, Jacques. (1981). *Positions* (A. Bass, Trans.). Chicago: University of Chicago Press.

Dillard, Annie. (1982). *Living by fiction.* New York: Harper & Row.

Dilthey, Wilhelm L. (1976). *Selected writings.* Cambridge: Cambridge University Press. (Original work published 1900)

Doig, Ivan. (1978). *This house of sky.* New York: Harcourt Brace.

Dolby-Stahl, Sandra K. (1985, January-April). A literary folkloristic methodology for the study of meaning in personal narrative. *Journal of Folklore Research, 22,* 45-70.

Dostoyevsky, Fyodor. (1950). *Crime and punishment.* New York: Vintage. (Original work published 1866)

Douglas, Jack D. (1985). *Creative interviewing.* Beverly Hills, CA: Sage.

Douglas, Jack D., & Johnson, John M. (Eds.). (1977). *Existential sociology.* New York: Cambridge University Press.

Downing, David B. (1987). Deconstruction's scruples: The politics of enlightened critique. *Diacritics, 17,* 66-81.

Du Bois, W. E. B. (1920). *Darkwater: Voices from within the veil.* New York: Schocken.

Faulkner, William. (1957). *The town.* New York: Vintage.

Faulkner, William. (1959). *The mansion.* New York: Vintage.

Faulkner, William. (1964). *The hamlet.* New York: Vintage. (Original work published 1940)

Faulkner, William. (1967). Address upon receiving the Nobel Prize for literature. In William Faulkner, *The portable Faulkner reader* (Rev. ed.; Malcolm Cowley, Ed.; pp. 723-724). New York: Viking.

Fiedler, Leslie. (1988). The Montana face. In William Kittredge & Annick Smith (Eds.), *The last best place: A Montana anthology* (pp. 744-752). Seattle: University of Washington Press.

Fielding, Nigel G., & Fielding, Jane L. (1986). *Linking data.* Beverly Hills, CA: Sage.

Fine, Michelle, Powell, Linda C., Weis, Lois, & Wong, Loonmun. (1997). Preface. In Michelle Fine, Linda C. Powell, Lois Weis, & Loonmun Wong (Eds.), *Off white: Readings on race, power and society* (pp. vii-xii). New York: Routledge.

Fish, Stanley. (1980). *Is there a text in this class? The authority of interpretive communities.* Cambridge, MA: Harvard University Press.

Fiske, John. (1994). Audiencing: Cultural practice and cultural studies. In Norman K. Denzin & Yvonna S. Lincoln (Eds.), *Handbook of qualitative research* (pp. 189-198). Thousand Oaks, CA: Sage.

Flick, Uwe. (1998). *An introduction to qualitative research: Theory, method and applications.* London: Sage.

Foucault, Michel. (1979). *Discipline and punish: The birth of the prison* (Alan M. Sheridan, Trans.). New York: Vintage.

Foucault, Michel. (1980). *Power/knowledge: Selected interviews and other writings, 1972-1977* (C. Gordon, Ed.; L. Marshall, J. Mepham, & K. Soper, Trans.). New York: Pantheon.

Foucault, Michel. (2000). *Power: Essential works of Foucault, 1954-1984* (Vol. 3; James D. Faubion, Ed.; Robert Hurley et al., Trans.). New York: New Press.

Freud, Sigmund. (1965). *The interpretation of dreams.* New York: Avon. (Original work published 1900)

Frow, John, & Morris, Meaghan. (2000). Cultural studies. In Norman K. Denzin & Yvonna S. Lincoln (Eds.), *Handbook of qualitative research* (2nd ed., pp. 315-346). Thousand Oaks, CA: Sage.

Gadamer, Hans-Georg. (1975). *Truth and method.* London: Sheed & Ward.

Gamson, Joshua. (2000). Sexualities, queer theory, and qualitative research. In Norman K. Denzin & Yvonna S. Lincoln (Eds.), *Handbook of qualitative research* (2nd ed., pp. 347-365). Thousand Oaks, CA: Sage.

Garfinkel, Harold. (1967). *Studies in ethnomethodology.* Englewood Cliffs, NJ: Prentice Hall.

Garfinkel, Harold, Lynch, Michael, & Livingston, Eric. (1981). The work of a discovering science construed with materials from the optically discovered pulsar. *Philosophy of the Social Sciences, 11,* 131-158.

Gayle, Addison, Jr. (1997). The black aesthetic. In Henry Louis Gates, Jr., & Nellie Y. McKay (Eds.), *The Norton anthology of African American literature* (pp. 1870-1877). New York: W. W. Norton. (Original work published 1971)

Geertz, Clifford. (1973a). Deep play: Notes on the Balinese cockfight. In Clifford Geertz, *The interpretation of cultures: Selected essays* (pp. 412-453). New York: Basic Books.

Geertz, Clifford. (1973b). Thick description: Toward an interpretive theory of culture. In Clifford Geertz, *The interpretation of cultures: Selected essays* (pp. 3-30). New York: Basic Books.

Geertz, Clifford. (1983). *Local knowledge: Further essays in interpretive anthropology.* New York: Basic Books.

Geertz, Clifford. (1988). *Works and lives: The anthropologist as author.* Stanford, CA: Stanford University Press.

Glasser, Theodore L. (Ed.). (1999). *The idea of public journalism.* New York: Guilford.

Goffman, Erving. (1959). *The presentation of self in everyday life.* Garden City, NY: Doubleday.

Goffman, Erving. (1961a). *Asylums: Essays on the social situation of mental patients and other inmates.* Garden City, NY: Doubleday.

Goffman, Erving. (1961b). *Encounters: Two studies in the sociology of interaction.* Indianapolis: Bobbs-Merrill.

Goffman, Erving. (1967). *Interaction ritual: Essays on face-to-face behavior.* Garden City, NY: Anchor.

Goffman, Erving. (1971). *Relations in public: Microstudies of the public order.* New York: Basic Books.

Goffman, Erving. (1974). *Frame analysis: An essay on the organization of experience.* New York: Harper & Row.

Goffman, Erving. (1981). *Forms of talk.* Philadelphia: University of Pennsylvania Press.

Goffman, Erving. (1983). The interaction order. *American Sociological Review, 48,* 1-17.

Graber, Doris, McQuail, Denis, & Norris, Pippa. (Eds.). (1998). *The politics of news: The news of politics.* Washington, DC: Congressional Quarterly Press.

Graetz, Rick. (1997, July-August). Sojourn to the sky: The Beartooth Highway. *Montana Magazine*, pp. 18-26.

Gubrium, Jaber F., & Holstein, James A. (2000). Analyzing interpretive practice. In Norman K. Denzin & Yvonna S. Lincoln (Eds.), *Handbook of qualitative research* (2nd ed., pp. 487-508). Thousand Oaks, CA: Sage.

Gupta, Akhil, & Ferguson, James. (1997). Discipline and practice: "The field" as site, method, and location in anthropology. In Akhil Gupta & James Ferguson (Eds.), *Anthropological locations: Boundaries and grounds of a field science* (pp. 1-46). Berkeley: University of California Press.

Halley, Jean. (2000). This I know: An exploration of remembering childhood and knowing now. *Qualitative Inquiry, 6,* 349-358.

Haraway, Donna J. (1991). *Simians, cyborgs, and women: The reinvention of nature.* New York: Routledge.

Harrington, Walt. (1992). *Crossings: A white man's journey into black America.* New York: HarperCollins.

Harrington, Walt. (1997a). Prologue: The job of remembering for the tribe. In Walt Harrington (Ed.), *Intimate journalism: The art and craft of reporting everyday life* (pp. vii-xvi). Thousand Oaks, CA: Sage.

Harrington, Walt. (1997b). A writer's essay: Seeking the extraordinary in the ordinary. In Walt Harrington (Ed.), *Intimate journalism: The art and craft of reporting everyday life* (pp. xvii-xlvi). Thousand Oaks, CA: Sage.

Heidegger, Martin. (1962). *Being and time.* New York: Harper & Row. (Original work published 1927)

Heidegger, Martin. (1982). *The basic problems of phenomenology.* Bloomington: Indiana University Press.

Henry, Jules. (1965). *Culture against man.* New York: Vintage.

Hill, Randall T. G. (1997). Performance and the "political anatomy" of pioneer Colorado. *Text and Performance Quarterly, 17,* 236-255.

Hollway, Wendy, & Jefferson, Tony. (2000). *Doing qualitative research differently.* London: Sage.

Holstein, James A., & Gubrium, Jaber F. (1995). *The active interview.* Thousand Oaks, CA: Sage.

Holstein, James A., & Gubrium, Jaber F. (2000). *The self we live by: Narrative identity in a postmodern world.* New York: Oxford University Press.

Hughes, Langston. (1962). *The ways of white folks.* New York: Vintage.

Husserl, Edmund. (1962). *Ideas: General introduction to pure phenomenology.* New York: Collier. (Original work published 1913)

Jackson, Michael. (1998). *Minima ethnographica: Intersubjectivity and the anthropological project.* Chicago: University of Chicago Press.

James, William. (1950). *The principles of psychology* (Vol. 1). New York: Dover. (Original work published 1890)

James, William. (1955). *Pragmatism and four essays from the meaning of truth.* New York: Humanities Press.

Jenkins, J. E. (1999, May 2). Narrating the action while taking part in it. *New York Times,* Arts and Leisure sec., pp. 9, 19.

Johnson, John M. (1977). Ethnomethodology and existential sociology. In Jack D. Douglas & John M. Johnson (Eds.), *Existential sociology* (pp. 153-173). New York: Cambridge University Press.

Johnson, John M., & Ferraro, Kathleen J. (1984). The victimized self: The case of battered women. In Joseph A. Kotarba & Andrea Fontana (Eds.), *The existential self in society* (pp. 119-130). Chicago: University of Chicago Press.

Jones, S. H. (1999). Torch. *Qualitative Inquiry, 5,* 235-250.

Joyce, James. (1976a). Counterparts. In James Joyce, *The Dubliners,* in James Joyce, *The portable James Joyce* (Harry Levin, Ed.; pp. 97-110). New York: Viking. (Original work published 1914)

Joyce, James. (1976b). *A portrait of the artist as a young man.* In James Joyce, *The portable James Joyce* (Harry Levin, Ed.; pp. 245-526). New York: Viking. (Original work published 1916)

Kafka, Franz. (1952). The metamorphosis. In Franz Kafka, *Selected short stories of Franz Kafka.* New York: Random House.

Kakutani, Michiko. (1987, December 13). John Huston's last legacy. *New York Times,* pp. 1, 50.

Karenga, Maulana. (1997). Black art: Mute matter given force and function. In Henry Louis Gates, Jr. & Nellie Y. McKay (Eds.), *The Norton anthology of African American literature* (pp. 1973-1977). New York: W. W. Norton. (Original work published 1972)

Kemmis, Stephen, & McTaggart, Robin. (2000). Participatory action research. In Norman K. Denzin & Yvonna S. Lincoln (Eds.), *Handbook of qualitative research* (2nd ed., pp. 567-605). Thousand Oaks, CA: Sage.

Kincheloe, Joe L., & McLaren, Peter. (2000). Rethinking critical theory and qualitative research. In Norman K. Denzin & Yvonna S. Lincoln (Eds.), *Handbook of qualitative research* (2nd ed., pp. 279-313). Thousand Oaks, CA: Sage.

Kittredge, William. (1987). *Owning it all.* San Francisco: Murray House.

Kittredge, William. (1994). *Hole in the sky: A memoir.* San Francisco: Murray House.

Kittredge, William. (1996). *Who owns the West?* San Francisco: Murray House.

Kotarba, Joseph A. (1998). Black men, black voices: The role of the producer in synthetic performance ethnography. *Qualitative Inquiry, 4,* 389-404.

Kotarba, Joseph A., & Fontana, Andrea. (Eds.). (1984). *The existential self in society.* Chicago: University of Chicago Press.

Kramer, Mark. (1995). Breakable rules for literary journalists. In Norman Sims & Mark Kramer (Eds.), *Literary journalism: A new collection of the best American nonfiction* (pp. 21-34). New York: Ballantine.

Krieger, Susan. (1996). *The family silver: Essays on relationships among women.* Berkeley: University of California Press.

Ladson-Billings, Gloria. (2000). Racialized discourses and ethnic epistemologies. In Norman K. Denzin & Yvonna S. Lincoln (Eds.), *Handbook of qualitative research* (2nd ed., pp. 257-277). Thousand Oaks, CA: Sage.

Langellier, Kristin M. (1999). Personal narrative, performance, performativity: Two or three things I know for sure. *Text and Performance Quarterly, 19,* 125-144.

Lather, Patti. (1991). *Getting smart: Feminist research and pedagogy with/in the postmodern.* New York: Routledge.

Lather, Patti, & Smithies, Chris. (1997). *Troubling the angels: Women living with HIV/AIDS.* Boulder, CO: Westview.

Lees, Gene. (1996). The poet: Bill Evans. In Robert Gottlieb (Ed.), *Reading jazz: A gathering of autobiography, reportage, and criticism from 1919 to now* (pp. 419-444). New York: Pantheon.

Lemert, Charles. (1997a). Goffman. In Charles Lemert & Ann Branaman (Eds.), *The Goffman reader* (pp. ix-xliii). Malden, MA: Blackwell.

Lemert, Charles. (1997b). *Postmodernism is not what you think*. Cambridge: Blackwell.

Levin, Harry. (1976). Editor's preface. In James Joyce, *The portable James Joyce* (Harry Levin, Ed.; pp. 17-18). New York: Viking.

Lieberson, Stanley. (1985). *Making it count: The improvement of social theory and research*. Berkeley: University of California Press.

Limerick, Patricia Nelson. (1997). The shadows of heaven itself. In William E. Reibsame (Ed.), *Atlas of the new West* (pp. 151-178). New York: W. W. Norton.

Lincoln, Yvonna S. (1997). Self, subject, audience, text: Living at the edge, writing in the margins. In William G. Tierney & Yvonna S. Lincoln (Eds.), *Representation and the text: Re-framing the narrative voice* (pp. 37-56). Albany: State University of New York Press.

Lincoln, Yvonna S., & Denzin, Norman K. (2000). The seventh moment: Out of the past. In Norman K. Denzin & Yvonna S. Lincoln (Eds.), *Handbook of qualitative research* (2nd ed., pp. 1047-1065). Thousand Oaks, CA: Sage.

Lincoln, Yvonna S., & Guba, Egon G. (1985). *Naturalistic inquiry*. Beverly Hills, CA: Sage.

Lincoln, Yvonna S., & Guba, Egon G. (2000). Paradigmatic controversies, contradictions, and emerging confluences. In Norman K. Denzin & Yvonna S. Lincoln (Eds.), *Handbook of qualitative research* (2nd ed., pp. 163-188). Thousand Oaks, CA: Sage.

Lindesmith, Alfred R. (1947). *Opiate addiction*. Bloomington, IN: Principia.

Lindesmith, Alfred R. (1952). Comment on W. S. Robinson's "The logical structure of analytic induction." *American Sociological Review, 17*, 492-493.

Lindesmith, Alfred R., Strauss, Anselm L., & Denzin, Norman K. (1999). *Social psychology* (8th ed.). Thousand Oaks, CA: Sage.

Lyotard, Jean-François. (1984). *The postmodern condition: A report on knowledge* (Geoff Bennington & Brian Massumi, Trans.). Minneapolis: University of Minnesota Press.

Madison, D. Soyini. (1999). Performing theory/embodied writing. *Text and Performance Quarterly, 19*, 107-124.

Maines, David R. (1993). Narrative's moment and sociology's phenomena: Toward a narrative sociology. *Sociological Quarterly, 34*, 17-38.

Majchrzak, Ann. (1984). *Methods for policy research*. Beverly Hills, CA: Sage.

Marcus, George E. (1998). *Ethnography through thick and thin*. Princeton, NJ: Princeton University Press.

McCall, Michal M. (2001). Three stories of loss and return. *Cultural Studies <=> Critical Methodologies, 1*(1), 50-61.

Mead, George Herbert. (1934). *Mind, self, and society: From the standpoint of a social behaviorist* (Charles W. Morris, Ed.). Chicago: University of Chicago Press.

Merleau-Ponty, Maurice. (1964). *The primacy of perception*. Evanston, IL: Northwestern University Press.

Merleau-Ponty, Maurice. (1968). *The visible and the invisible*. Evanston, IL: Northwestern University Press.

Merleau-Ponty, Maurice. (1973). *The prose of the world*. Evanston, IL: Northwestern University Press.

Mienczakowski, Jim. (1995). The reconstruction of ethnography into theater with emancipatory potential. *Qualitative Inquiry, 1*, 360-375.

Mills, C. Wright. (1959). *The sociological imagination*. New York: Oxford University Press.

Mills, C. Wright. (1963). *Power, politics, and people: The collected essays of C. Wright Mills* (Irving Louis Horowitz, Ed.). New York: Ballantine.

Olesen, Virginia L. (2000). Feminisms and qualitative research at and into the millennium. In Norman K. Denzin & Yvonna S. Lincoln (Eds.), *Handbook of qualitative research* (2nd ed., pp. 215-255). Thousand Oaks, CA: Sage.

Ortner, Sherry B. (1997a). Introduction. In Sherry B. Ortner (Ed.), The fate of "culture": Geertz and beyond [Special issue]. *Representations, 59,* 1-13.

Ortner, Sherry B. (1997b). Thick resistance: Death and the cultural construction of agency in Himalayan mountaineering. In Sherry B. Ortner (Ed.), The fate of "culture": Geertz and beyond [Special issue]. *Representations, 59,* 135-162.

Paget, Marianne A. (1993). *A complex sorrow* (Marjorie L. DeVault, Ed.). Philadelphia: Temple University Press.

Peirce, Charles Sanders. (1934). *Collected papers of Charles Sanders Peirce* (Vols. 5-6). Cambridge, MA: Harvard University Press.

Peirce, Charles Sanders. (1963). *Collected papers of Charles Sanders Peirce* (Vols. 7-8). Cambridge, MA: Harvard University Press.

Perinbanayagam, R. S. (1985). *Signifying acts.* Carbondale: Southern Illinois University Press.

Phelan, Peggy. (1998). Introduction: The ends of performance. In Peggy Phelan & Jill Lane (Eds.), *The ends of performance* (pp. 1-22). New York: New York University Press.

Phelan, Peggy, & Lane, Jill. (Eds.). (1998). *The ends of performance.* New York: New York University Press.

Pike, Kenneth. (1954). *Language in relation to a unified theory of the structure of human behavior* (Vol. 1). Glendale, CA: Summer Institute of Linguistics.

Pollock, Della. (1998). Performing writing. In Peggy Phelan & Jill Lane (Eds.), *The ends of performance* (pp. 73-193). New York: New York University Press.

Psathas, George. (1995). *Conversation analysis.* Thousand Oaks, CA: Sage.

Rabinow, Paul. (1986). Representations are social facts: Modernity and post-modernity in anthropology. In James Clifford & George E. Marcus (Eds.), *Writing culture: The poetics and politics of ethnography* (pp. 234-261). Berkeley: University of California Press.

Raines, Howell. (1986, November 30). [Review of the book *Bearing the cross: Martin Luther King Jr. and the Southern Christian Leadership Conference,* by David J. Garrow]. *New York Review of Books,* pp. 33-34.

Reason, Peter. (1993). Sacred experience and sacred science. *Journal of Management Inquiry, 2,* 10-27.

Reason, Peter. (Ed.). (1994). *Participation in human inquiry.* London: Sage.

Red Lodge Chamber of Commerce. (1982). *Festival of Nations, Red Lodge, Montana* [brochure]. Red Lodge, MT: Author.

Richardson, Laurel. (1997). *Fields of play: Constructing an academic life.* New Brunswick, NJ: Rutgers University Press.

Richardson, Laurel. (1999). Paradigms lost. *Symbolic Interaction, 22,* 79-91.

Richardson, Laurel. (2000). Writing: A method of inquiry. In Norman K. Denzin & Yvonna S. Lincoln (Eds.), *Handbook of qualitative research* (2nd ed., pp. 923-948). Thousand Oaks, CA: Sage.

Ricoeur, Paul. (1979). The model of the text: Meaningful action considered as a text. In Paul Rabinow & William M. Sullivan (Eds.), *Interpretive social science: A reader* (pp. 73-101). Berkeley: University of California Press.

Ricoeur, Paul. (1985). *Time and narrative* (Vol. 2). Chicago: University of Chicago Press.

Rofel, Lisa B. (1994). Yearnings: Televisual love and melodramatic politics in contemporary China. *American Ethnologist, 21,* 700-722.

Ronai, Carol Rambo. (1998). Sketching with Derrida: An ethnography of a researcher/ erotic dancer. *Qualitative Inquiry, 4,* 405-420.

Ronai, Carol Rambo. (1999). The next night *sous rature:* Wrestling with Derrida's mimesis. *Qualitative Inquiry, 5,* 114-129.

Rosaldo, Renato. (1984). Grief and a headhunter's rage: On the cultural force of emotions. In Edward M. Bruner (Ed.), *Text, play, and story: The construction and reconstruction of self and society* (pp. 178-198). Washington, DC: American Ethnological Society.

Rosaldo, Renato. (1986). Ilongot hunting as story and experience. In Victor W. Turner & Edward M. Bruner (Eds.), *The anthropology of experience* (pp. 97-138). Urbana: University of Illinois Press.

Rosen, Jay. (1994). Making things more public: On the political responsibility of the media intellectual. *Critical Studies in Mass Communication, 11,* 362-388.

Ryan, Katherine E., Greene, Jennifer, Lincoln, Yvonna S., Mathison, Sandra, & Mertens, Donna M. (1998). Advantages and challenges of using inclusive evaluation approaches in evaluation practice. *American Journal of Evaluation, 19*(1), 101-122.

Ryle, Gilbert. (1968). *The thinking of thoughts* (University Lecture No. 18). Saskatoon: University of Saskatchewan.

Sams, Ferrol. (1994). *Epiphany.* New York: Penguin.

Sartre, Jean-Paul. (1948). *The psychology of imagination.* New York: Philosophical Library.

Sartre, Jean-Paul. (1956). *Being and nothingness.* New York: Philosophical Library. (Original work published 1943)

Sartre, Jean-Paul. (1963). *Search for a method.* New York: Alfred A. Knopf.

Sartre, Jean-Paul. (1981). *The family idiot: Gustave Flaubert, 1821-1857* (Vol. 1). Chicago: University of Chicago Press.

Scheler, Max. (1961). *Ressentiment* (L. Coser, Ed.; W. H. Holdeim, Trans.). New York: Free Press. (Original work published 1912)

Schutz, Alfred. (1964). *Collected papers: Vol. 2. Studies in social theory.* The Hague: Martinus Nijhoff.

Schwandt, Thomas A. (1994). Constructivist, interpretivist approaches to human inquiry. In Norman K. Denzin & Yvonna S. Lincoln (Eds.), *Handbook of qualitative research* (pp. 118-137). Thousand Oaks, CA: Sage.

Schwandt, Thomas A. (1999). On understanding understanding. *Qualitative Inquiry, 5,* 451-464.

Schwandt, Thomas A. (2000). Three epistemological stances for qualitative inquiry. In Norman K. Denzin & Yvonna S. Lincoln (Eds.), *Handbook of qualitative research* (2nd ed., pp. 189-213). Thousand Oaks, CA: Sage.

Searle, John R. (1969). *Speech acts.* New York: Cambridge University Press.

Silverman, David. (1985). *Qualitative methodology and sociology: Describing the social world.* Brookfield, VT: Gower.

Simonelli, Jeanne. (2000). Field school in Chiapas. *Qualitative Inquiry, 6,* 104-106.

Sims, Norman. (1995). The art of literary journalism. In Norman Sims & Mark Kramer (Eds.), *Literary journalism: A new collection of the best American nonfiction* (pp. 3-19). New York: Ballantine.

Smith, Anna Deavere. (1993). *Fires in the mirror: Crown Heights, Brooklyn, and other identities.* Garden City, NY: Anchor.

Smith, Dorothy E. (1989). Sociological theory: Methods of writing patriarchy. In Ruth A. Wallace (Ed.), *Feminism and sociological theory* (pp. 34-64). Newbury Park, CA: Sage.

Smith, Dorothy E. (1993). High noon in Textland: A critique of Clough. *Sociological Quarterly, 34,* 183-192.

Smith, John K., & Deemer, Deborah K. (2000). The problem of criteria in the age of relativism. In Norman K. Denzin & Yvonna S. Lincoln (Eds.), *Handbook of qualitative research* (2nd ed., pp. 877-896). Thousand Oaks, CA: Sage.

Stake, Robert E. (1978). The case-study method of social inquiry. *Educational Researcher, 7*(2), 5-8.

Stake, Robert E. (2000). Case studies. In Norman K. Denzin & Yvonna S. Lincoln (Eds.), *Handbook of qualitative research* (2nd ed., pp. 435-454). Thousand Oaks, CA: Sage.

Strauss, Anselm L. (1959). *Mirrors and masks: The search for identity.* Glencoe, IL: Free Press.

Strauss, Anselm L. (1987). *Qualitative analysis for social scientists.* New York: Cambridge University Press.

Stringer, Ernest T. (1996). *Action research.* Thousand Oaks, CA: Sage.

Sudnow, David. (1978). *Ways of the hand.* New York: Alfred A. Knopf.

Sudnow, David. (1979). *Talk's body.* New York: Alfred A. Knopf.

Taussig, Michael. (1993). *Mimesis and alterity: A particular history of the senses.* New York: Routledge.

Tedlock, Barbara. (2000). Ethnography and ethnographic representation. In Norman K. Denzin & Yvonna S. Lincoln (Eds.), *Handbook of qualitative research* (2nd ed., pp. 455-486). Thousand Oaks, CA: Sage.

Thomas, Dylan. (1964). *Adventures in the skin trade and other stories.* New York: New Directions. (Original work published 1938)

Thompson, Paul. (1978). *Voices of the past: Oral history.* Oxford: Oxford University Press.

Tierney, William G. (2000). Undaunted courage: Life history and the postmodern challenge. In Norman K. Denzin & Yvonna S. Lincoln (Eds.), *Handbook of qualitative research* (2nd ed., pp. 537-553). Thousand Oaks, CA: Sage.

Titon, Jeff Todd. (1980). The life story. *Journal of American Folklore, 93,* 276-292.

Turner, Victor W. (1986a). *The anthropology of performance.* New York: Performing Arts Journal Publications.

Turner, Victor W. (1986b). Dewey, Dilthey, and drama: An essay in the anthropology of experience. In Victor W. Turner & Edward M. Bruner (Eds.), *The anthropology of experience* (pp. 3-30). Urbana: University of Illinois Press.

Ulmer, Gregory. (1989). *Teletheory: Grammatology in an age of video.* New York: Routledge.

Vaughan, Diane. (1986). *Uncoupling: Turning points in intimate relationships.* New York: Oxford University Press.

West, Cornel. (1993). Foreword. In Anna Deavere Smith, *Fires in the mirror: Crown Heights, Brooklyn, and other identities* (pp. xvii-xxii). Garden City, NY: Anchor.

Wilkinson, Charles. (1997). Paradise revisited. In William E. Reibsame (Ed.), *Atlas of the new West* (pp. 15-150). New York: W. W. Norton.

Willis, Paul, & Trondman, Mats. (2000). Manifesto for *Ethnography. Ethnography, 1,* 5-16.

Wittgenstein, Ludwig. (1922). *Tractacus logico-philosophicus.* London: Routledge & Kegan Paul.

Wolfe, Tom. (1973). The new journalism. In Tom Wolfe & E. W. Johnson (Eds.), *The new journalism: An anthology* (pp. 1-52). New York: Harper & Row.

Name Index

Subject Index

performing Montana, 24
Reflexive participant observation. *See* Participant observation
Reflexive performance texts, 12, 16, 19-20
Reformist movement, ix
Relationship:
   client-public, 12
   differences and, 4
   moral community and, 4-5
Relativism, 3
Representational adequacy, 11, 98
Representational forms, 7-9, 16
Researchers:
   advocacy, position of, 5
   positivism and, 43-44
   research subjects and, 96-97
   researched and, moral dialogue, 5
   sophisticated rigor and, 42
   types of, 42-43
   viewpoint of, 3, 32
   See also Ethnography; Interpretive process; Interpretive research
Resistance, 5
Responsibility, personal/communal, 4
Revisionism, 3
Rituals, 38-39, 40

Sacredness, 5
Science:
   biography/inquiry and, 46-47
   interpretive perspective and, 44-46
   See also Social science
Self-story construction, xi, 58-59, 60, 61
Semiotic analysis, xi, 77
Seventh moment of inquiry, x
   civic transformation, 9-11
   moral criticism, taking sides and, 5-6
   moral/ethical evaluative criteria, 4-5
   performance texts, 12-15, 16-20
   Red Lodge, Montana, 20-24
   representational forms in, 7-9
   writing norms, 11-12
   See also Interpretive interactionism
Situated interpretation, 52, 85
   gaining access, 89-90
   language/meanings, 91-96
   local/global ethnography and, 85-87
   researcher-newcomer/knowing subject, 96-97
   temporal mapping, 87-89
Social action, 5

betterment and, 6
civic journalism and, 10-11
performance texts and, 16
policy-making research and, 42-43
Social constructionism:
   knowledge and, 51
   narrative forms and, 7-9, 59
Social criticism, 5
Social exchange theory, 73
Social media, 5
Social moral philosophy, 42
Social organization:
   difference, relationships of, 4
   power and, 4, 14-15
   processual ritual model of, 38-39
Social programs:
   community services, 3
   effectiveness of, 2
Social responsibility. *See* Social action
Social science, ix
   critical/antifoundational, 3-4
   experience-distant concepts, 103
   feminist standpoint theorists and, 45-46
   generalizability in, 46-47, 63-64, 98
   interpretive perspective in, 44-46
   minimalist/performative, 15
   myths and, 150
   narrative in, 58-59
   textual convention/style in, 150-151
   thin description in, 102-103, 104-106
Social world:
   improvement in, 6
   interpretation/understanding and, 2-3
   researcher and, 3-4
   self and, 58-59
   truths of, 12
   See also Situated interpretation
Sociological imagination, 70-71
Sociology, x-xi
   performative ethnography and, 15
   positivistic/scientific, 44-46
   research in, 43-44
Sophisticated rigor, 42
Speech acts, theory of, 20
Standpoints, 3, 6
Statistical evaluations, 2
Stereotyping, 6, 11
Storytelling:
   allegorical, 12
   journalistic case studies, 7-9
   mystories, 16, 59

About the Author

Norman K. Denzin is Distinguished Professor of Communications, College of Communications Scholar, and Research Professor of Communications, Sociology and Humanities at the University of Illinois, Urbana-Champaign. He is the author of numerous books, including *Reading Race: Hollywood and the Cinema of Racial Violence, Interpretive Ethnography: Ethnographic Practices for the 21st Century, The Cinematic Society: The Voyeur's Gaze, Images of Postmodern Society, The Research Act: A Theoretical Introduction to Sociological Methods, Interpretive Interactionism, Hollywood Shot by Shot, The Recovering Alcoholic,* and *The Alcoholic Self,* which won the Charles Cooley Award from the Society for the Study of Symbolic Interaction in 1988. In 1997 he was awarded the George Herbert Mead Award from the Society for the Study of Symbolic Interaction. He is past editor of the *Sociological Quarterly,* coeditor of both editions of the *Handbook of Qualitative Research,* coeditor of *Qualitative Inquiry,* editor of the journal *Cultural Studies—Critical Methodologies,* and editor of the series *Studies in Symbolic Interaction.*

CPSIA information can be obtained at www.ICGtesting.com
Printed in the USA
239838LV00001B/2/P